EURO DISNEY: THE UNOFFICIAL

Euro Disney

THE MAINSTREAM UnOfficial GUIDE

TANIA ALEXANDER

EDINBURGH AND LONDON

ACKNOWLEDGEMENT
I'd like to thank P&O European Ferries for helping us in our research for this book.

All prices quoted are as accurate as possible at time of going to press

Copyright © Tania Alexander 1992

All rights reserved

This edition 1993

The moral right of the author has been asserted
First published in Great Britain in 1992 by
MAINSTREAM PUBLISHING COMPANY (EDINBURGH) LTD
7 Albany Street
EDINBURGH EH1 3UG

ISBN 1 855158 513 3

No part of this publication may be reproduced or transmitted in any form or by any means without the permission in writing from the publisher, except by a reviewer who wishes to quote brief passages in connection with a review written for insertion in a magazine, newspaper or broadcast.

A catalogue record for this book is available from the British Library

Phototypeset in 11 on 13pt Century Roman by Intype, London
Printed and bound in Great Britain by
BPCC Hazells Ltd
Member of BPCC Ltd

To Stuart, with all my love

IMPORTANT NOTES

Trademarks
All characters and attractions mentioned in this book are the property of the Walt Disney Company Limited. The following names and terms included in this volume are Walt Disney registered trademarks and as such all rights to their use is courtesy of the Walt Disney Company Limited.

Euro Disney	Frontierland
Euro Disneyland	Discoveryland
Audio-Animatronics	Adventure Isle
Magic Kingdom	Festival Disney
Walt Disney	Adventureland
Disneyland	Caption EO
Walt Disney World	Fantasyland

Prices
Please note that all prices are correct at time of publication. The publisher and author cannot accept responsibility for any changes which may occur.

Telephoning France
The international dialing code from the UK to France is 010 33 followed by the number (8 digits). For the city of Paris and the Greater Paris Area, dial 010 33 1 + 8 digits.

Contents

Foreword	1
Introduction	3

CHAPTER ONE
What to Expect from a Holiday at Euro Disney — 9

CHAPTER TWO
What will it Cost? — 17

CHAPTER THREE
Booking your Holiday — 25

CHAPTER FOUR
Where to Stay — 35

CHAPTER FIVE
The Layout of Euro Disney — 63

CHAPTER SIX
Reviews of Rides and Attractions — 79

CHAPTER SEVEN
The Unofficial Restaurant Guide — 127

CHAPTER EIGHT
The Unofficial Shopping Guide — 151

CHAPTER NINE
The Unofficial Entertainment Guide — 173

CHAPTER TEN
The Unofficial Guided Tours   181

CHAPTER ELEVEN
Excursions   213

CHAPTER TWELVE
The Unofficial Disney Quiz   249

CHAPTER THIRTEEN
Where to Find your Favourite Characters   259
Readers' Response   266

INDEX   267

Foreword

Why "Unofficial"?

This book is an "unofficial" guide to Euro Disney. This means that it has not been endorsed in any way by the Walt Disney Corporation, so we have been free to give an unbiased consumer account of everything the resort has to offer. We have not been on any fancy press trips, been whisked to the front of the queues like VIPs, or been given special accommodation in any of the hotels. All our research at Euro Disney has been done as paying customers – so as you will be doing, we have been looking for value for money and good service.

That is not to say that this book is a negative or critical attack on Euro Disney. I am and always will be a great fan and am extremely impressed by this new European resort.

The aim of this book is to help you make the most of your stay. So if I have felt a restaurant or hotel is not up to scratch, I have said so. Or if any of my reviewers have been disappointed with a particular ride, this will be made quite clear. Equally, if something is an attraction not to be missed or a restaurant that is well worth sampling, you will be the first to know about it.

Armed with this book, you should have all the

EURO DISNEY: THE MAINSTREAM UNOFFICIAL GUIDE

"unofficial" and insider information to make your stay truly magical and memorable.

Introduction

If you're planning a trip to Euro Disney, you will want to make sure that your holiday runs as smoothly as possible so you can enjoy every minute of this magical world. This guide is for everyone who wants to get the best out of their visit to Euro Disney.

Whether it's just for a day or a week-long blitz, EURO DISNEY: THE MAINSTREAM UNOFFICIAL GUIDE gives you a step-by-step guide on how to plan your holiday, from booking to actually touring the resort and the surrounding area. The book tells you exactly what to expect from a holiday at Euro Disney, answering questions such as what it will cost, how long the queues are and how is the place run. Written from a consumer journalist's point of view, this guidebook shows you how to get the best value out of Euro Disney.

Let me say right from the start that I'm as crazy about the magical world of Disney as the rest of you. As a child, I believed that elephants could fly, that if I told fibs, my nose would sprout, and that all jungle animals could calypso. I saw all the films, read the books, bought the records. My parents couldn't tear me away from the television when a Disney programme was showing.

Disney's ability to both entertain and to educate is unique. Their films are timeless, rich in detail and vivid in imagery. You are watching a film, and then suddenly, there you are in their world. Disney have an unbeatable talent to educate, inform and stimulate a youngster's imagination.

But then Disney is as much for adults as it is for children. In fact, about three-quarters of visitors to the Disney parks in the States are over 18, and Disney World has replaced Niagara Falls as America's top honeymoon destination. Whatever your age, you will love it.

Even the most hardened cynics cannot fail to be touched by the magic of their creations. When I was a child, it was too expensive to go to Disney World in the States. We had to be content with the cinema and picture books. It was not until I was in my twenties that I made my first visit to Disney in the US. I had just left university and prided myself in being an experienced traveller. I thought I was too old and sophisticated to be going to a theme park, but as soon as I walked through those gates and strolled down Main Street USA, my scepticism evaporated and everything I had loved about Disney as a child came flooding back. This is fantasy land that lets us all be Peter Pan.

The Disney theme parks bring to life the stories we all know so well from the world of cinema. Instead of seeing Mickey Mouse and his friends on a screen, there they are before you. Instead of reading about Peter Pan, you can actually take to the skies yourself for a flight over London and Never-Never-Land. And then there is the unique Star Tours adventure, a simulated journey into space. The first time I tried the latter I was so

INTRODUCTION

terrified and convinced that my plight was "real" that I very nearly had to pull the Emergency Stop handle! This ability to project you into their adventures is something that Disney calls "imagineering" and no-one does it better. Love it or hate it, a trip to Disney can never be an objective experience. You are involved from the moment you walk through those gates.

The Disney parks are a world on their own and an escape from the seedier realities of life. In Disney parks you do not see any litter, graffiti or lager louts (alcohol is not allowed in the park).

Euro Disney, located 32 kilometres east of Paris, has opened up the magical world of Disney for thousands of Europeans. At long last, all the colour and excitement of Disney is on your doorstep. You no longer have to contend with long and tiring flights halfway across the world as you can get to Euro Disney within an hour or two by air from the UK. When the Channel tunnel opens in 1994, the high-speed TGV trains are scheduled to stop at Euro Disney, and will enable you to travel direct there from London in three and a half hours. It is such an easy place to get to that a short two-day trip or even a one-day stop-over is quite feasible.

Disney is renowned for its superb organisation and management skills. But even in their world, you will find that you still have to queue for the most popular attractions. There's no magic formula, even here! That's where this guide can help. We have carefully planned a selection of Unofficial Guided Tours to help you avoid the worst of the queues and see the best of the attractions.

We have devised tours for both adults, and families with young children. Got just a day? Fine. Follow our Whirlwind Tours and you'll find you can pack in all the best rides with time for lunch in between.

Of course, we do recommend you spend more time exploring the wonders of Disney, so if possible, stay for longer and enjoy our special Two-day Tours and sample all the attractions with plenty of time to try out your favourites again.

If you're lucky enough to be spending a week or more at Euro Disney, you'll find here a complete guide to all that the site has to offer as well as the many attractions of the surrounding countryside. We have included a special chapter on excursions, detailing all sorts of day trips accessible from Euro Disney. Why not visit a local vineyard (the Champagne region is only a short drive away), spend a day in the old city of Chantilly or enjoy the white-knuckle rides at the local French theme park, Parc Asterix? We've included details of all sorts of local sporting facilities from windsurfing on a nearby lake to horseriding in the forests of Fontainebleau. Or why not take a trip to the magical capital of Paris – it's only a half-hour train ride away so we have included details of all the highlights that you may want to see in a day's excursion to the French capital.

All the rides and attractions at Euro Disney have been graded (* to *****). Similarly, we have reviewed and graded all the restaurants, shops and entertainment.

As accommodation is such an important part of any holiday, we have carefully reviewed all the hotels on site, as well as finding other places in the area for you to stay at, ranging from cheap bed and breakfasts to a luxury château in the Champagne region which flies you direct to Disney by helicopter.

Throughout the book, we have put an emphasis on getting value for money so that you will find many ways to cut the cost of your holiday from booking cheaper accommodation to eating at the more reasonably priced restaurants.

We've also included details of the best route to take if you are driving, and a special Unofficial Disney Quiz to entertain all the family. Finally, in Chapter Thirteen, we tell you where to find your children's favourite characters in the park.

Whether this is your first visit to Disney or your fifth, I hope this book will tell you everything you need to know and helps make your stay a truly magical experience.

CHAPTER ONE

WHAT TO EXPECT FROM A HOLIDAY AT EURO DISNEY

This chapter gives you some background information to Euro Disney and answers the sort of questions you may ask before booking a holiday.

APRIL 1992: MICKEY ARRIVED IN EUROPE!

Disney are veterans in the field of theme parks. The first Disney resort, Disneyland, opened in 1955 in California and on its opening day, Walt Disney called it "the happiest place on earth". Today, he would have to call it "one of" the happiest places on earth as there are now four Disney pleasure parks, spread over three continents. Mickey Mouse is set to rule the world.

Walt Disney World opened in Florida in 1971 and Tokyo Disneyland began operating in 1983. Euro Disney opened just outside Paris in 1992 and is the fourth and latest Disney resort. Based on the original Magic Kingdom at Disneyland in California, the European park has also been influenced by the Florida and Tokyo parks.

A CENTRAL EUROPEAN LOCATION

Euro Disney is located 32km east of Paris in the Marne-la-Vallée on what was originally a 5,000-acre site of flat beet fields. It is an ideal location for a European Disney resort as it is located along the A4 expressway that runs from Paris to Strasbourg and is therefore easily accessible from most central European countries.

Although you never really feel as though you are in France when you are inside the theme park, the atmosphere is very cosmopolitan with tourists from all over Europe.

WHAT TO EXPECT FROM A HOLIDAY AT EURO DISNEY

HI HO, HI HO, IT'S OFF TO WORK WE GO ...

The construction of Euro Disney began in earnest in August 1988 and involved the removal of more than four million cubic metres of earth and the planting of hundreds of thousands of trees. In December 1990, Espace Euro Disney, an information centre, opened to the public and people arrived in their coachloads for a sneak preview of the resort.

The opening of Euro Disney has created a need for over 12,000 workers, the majority of whom are French, although Disney have recruited staff from all over Europe including the UK. Disney employees are called "cast members" and nearly 4,500 star in the park's attractions, shops and restaurants, while 6,000 offer Disney smiles and hospitality to "guests" in the resort hotels and a further 1,500 work "backstage" providing administrative support.

The Euro Disney Casting Center opened on 1 September 1991. Disney were clearly looking for a certain type of employee. "The main qualities necessary for all cast members are friendliness, warmth and a genuine interest in people," they said.

"Cast members" have to be bilingual (French and English) and prepared to follow strict and disciplinarian rules. The female "cast" have to wear "appropriate underwear" – fishnet stockings and suspenders are out, as are earrings larger than a penny piece, obviously dyed hair, mini-skirts and make-up that does not look natural. They are also not allowed to wear more than one ring on each hand. Similarly, the male "cast" are not allowed visible tattoos, long hair, beards or moustaches. Both sexes have to wear deodorant and not be overweight.

WILL THEY SPEAK ENGLISH?

All the cast members in the park are supposed to speak English. You can tell at a glance what languages cast members speak as these are displayed by badges of national flags on their jackets.

STANDARDS

The general standard of professionalism at Euro Disney is superb. Everything was ready and working on the opening day. The staff have been trained in the American cheery "Have a nice day!" style, although this seems a little incongruous sometimes coming from European mouths!

CLEANLINESS

Euro Disney is a world without litter or graffiti. Everything is kept spotlessly clean from the roads in the park to the floors in the restaurants. Litter attendants are dressed all in white and seem to pick any rubbish or cigarette ends up before they even reach the ground!

THE WEATHER

Euro Disney is open 365 days a year. Unless you go in the height of the summer you should be prepared for cool and wet weather. There is nothing worse than sitting shivering on the rides or queuing in the rain with no protection. Even though Euro Disney has more covered areas than the parks in the States you can get very cold and wet there and some exposure to the elements is inevitable. Make sure you pack some warm waterproof clothing. Also see Chapter Ten for the best rides and attractions to try in the rain.

MORE THAN A THEME PARK

Euro Disney has been created as a giant pleasure resort, a place you go to for a holiday rather than a day trip. Unlike other local theme parks such as Parc Asterix (*see page 222*) Euro Disney has on-site hotels which are "attractions" in themselves, all with health clubs, shops and restaurants and based on themes inspired by a particular American time or place. Once you are in the resort, there is no need to step outside, as everything from banking facilities to swimming pools, golf and tennis is on-site.

WILL THE CHILDREN COPE WITH THE RIDES?

Children of all ages will enjoy Euro Disney. Little children and toddlers will probably appreciate the characters more than the rides. Some rides such as Star Tours and Big Thunder Mountain have height restrictions and are more suited to the over-sevens.

WHAT WILL THE QUEUES BE LIKE?

There are always queues for the most popular attractions such as Big Thunder Mountain and Peter Pan's Flight. This book, however, will help you avoid the worst queues and so spend more time on the rides. Chapter Ten outlines detailed tours to help you minimise the time spent queuing.

FACILITIES FOR DISABLED PEOPLE

Euro Disney has been designed with disabled people in mind. All the hotels have special rooms and most of the restaurants have special toilets.

People with wheelchairs are given priority on all the rides. Disney's "Guest Special Services Guide" (available from the Main Entrance and City Hall in Main Street USA) outlines special access to attractions, restaurants and shops. Wheelchairs can be hired in Main Street USA.

Complimentary use of audio cassettes and portable tape players is provided at City Hall for sight-impaired visitors. Guide dogs are allowed in most of the park. Complimentary use of a special telephone device is provided at City Hall for hearing-impaired visitors.

HOW DOES EURO DISNEY DIFFER FROM THE AMERICAN PARKS?

Although Euro Disney is based on the original Disneyland's Magic Kingdom, there are aspects about this new park that are distinctly European. Sleeping Beauty's castle has become the Château de la Belle au Bois Dormant and many people think it is the most beautiful of all the Disney castles, perhaps influenced by the French art of building châteaux. The futuristic theme land, Discoveryland, is unique to Euro Disney and stars European figures such as Leonardo da Vinci, H. G. Wells and Jules Verne.

Euro Disney is also smaller than the American parks. Euro Disney covers 5,000 acres (one-fifth of the size of Paris) compared to the 28,000 acres of Disney World – which is twice the size of Manhattan. In keeping with European standards, the size of hotel rooms is also smaller at Euro Disney. Most of the food at Euro Disney is American rather than French.

HOW LONG SHOULD I GO FOR?

As you will see from our Whirlwind Tour (*page 182*) it is perfectly possible to see the best of Euro Disney in one day. To make the most of the resort you really need two or three days.

WHAT SHOULD I PACK?

Your most important item is a comfortable pair of trainers or walking shoes, as you will be on your feet for much of the day. Anoraks, hats and waterproof clothing are a must in winter and it is best to be prepared for wet, chilly weather for most of the year – apart from summer. Money belts are a much safer option than handbags. And don't forget your camera, plenty of film and a pencil so you can do the quiz in Chapter 12!

FUTURE PLANS

The long-term development of Euro Disney is planned up to 2017. Over the next few years there will be more campsites, 13,000 more hotel rooms, a convention centre, single family homes, a water park, expansion of the golf course and a second course. In 1994 the highspeed TGV rail network will be linked with a station at Euro Disney Resort and movie and television production facilities will be opened. A second theme park, Disney MGM Studios-Europe, is scheduled to open in 1995. By the year 2000 the workforce at Euro Disney is estimated to be about 25,000 increasing to 30,000 by 2017.

DISNEYSPEAK

Finally, when you go to Euro Disney, you will soon notice that this magical land has a language all of its own. Here are some special Disney words and their meanings:

Adult – anyone over the age of 12 is an adult and pays the full entrance fee.

Cabins – mobile homes in Camp Davy Crockett.

Cast members – Disney employees.

Disney spirit – Big smiles and the cast's ability to never look flustered.

Disney University – Training centre for cast.

Guests – paying visitors to Disney.

Guest relations – information desk.

Guest rooms – hotel rooms.

Members of the Disney Participant Family – Sponsors.

Pre-Entertainment Area – Queues.

Retail Entertainment Centres – Shops.

CHAPTER TWO

WHAT WILL IT COST?

So, you've decided that you want to go to Euro Disney but are not sure exactly what it is going to cost. This chapter runs through everything you are likely to have to pay for during a holiday in Euro Disney, from the initial travel package to extras such as coffee and beers. By following our guidelines you will be able to get better value for money and be able to budget more accurately before you even set off.

17

WILL IT COST MORE THAN A HOLIDAY IN THE STATES?

There have been many reports about how expensive Euro Disney is, and the prices are indeed higher than in the States. You pay about £8 more just to get in, and hotel, restaurant and bar prices are all inflated this side of the Atlantic. But as you'll probably stay only for a couple of days, it need not put you out of pocket, particularly if you follow the guidelines in this book. In fact, the theme park is designed for short stays and a family of four can have a great day out for 750F.

ACCOMMODATION

If you are on a tight budget, the cheapest way to stay at Euro Disney is in a local campsite, motel or auberge (*see Chapter Four for suggested places*). You should be able to find a room in a local motel for under 150F per night. There are tour operators selling packages using cheap accommodation off-site but check if they include guaranteed entry to the theme park as otherwise you will have to pay each day to get in.

The Disney accommodation is superb both in quality and atmosphere and hotel prices start at 550F for a room per night. The top hotel is Hotel Disneyland which is located right at the entrance to the park, overlooking Main Street USA. Prices in this hotel start at 1300F per night.

Another alternative is to stay in Paris itself and commute to Euro Disney on the RER metro network (45 minutes from Arc de Triomphe).

If you are looking for luxury accommodation outside Euro Disney there are several beautiful châteaux in the nearby countryside. A room in a château will cost you from about 450F per night.

See Chapter Four for full details of where to stay and hotel reviews.

THE MORE THE MERRIER!

It is more economical to travel as a family or group of four than as a couple or a single person, as all the Euro Disney accommodation and most of the accommodation off-site charges for the room regardless of how many people occupy it.

If you are travelling on your own, it should be cheaper to stay outside the resort.

SHOULD I BOOK INDEPENDENTLY OR AS PART OF A PACKAGE?

It usually works out cheaper to buy a package which includes an entrance pass to the park. If you book a hotel room directly with Euro Disney you have to buy your entry ticket separately. See Chapter Three for full details about booking your holiday.

HOW MUCH WILL A PACKAGE COST?

A typical cheap package costs from £77 per person for two nights at the Santa Fe hotel with P&O European Ferries Holidays. This is based on a family of two adults and two children sharing a room and includes ferry crossings, accommodation and guaranteed free entry to the park for the length of your stay. See pages 30–1 for a full list of tour operators.

WHAT WILL IT COST ME TO GET THERE?

The cheapest ways to get to Euro Disney are by coach or self-drive (with four people in the car). If you are staying on-site you will not need a car. Self-drive is ideal if you plan to extend your stay by touring the area.

HOW MUCH WILL THE PETROL AND TOLLS COST?

Depending on your make of car you should be able to drive to Euro Disney (less than 200 miles from Calais) on a full tank of petrol).

The quickest way to get there is on the autoroutes. Toll charges are 84F from Calais to Euro Disney.

CAR HIRE

If you want to explore the local countryside (see Chapter Eleven: Excursions) you can hire a car. Europcar has an office near the Hotel Santa Fe at Euro Disney. They charge between 710F and 3560F for 2 days.

HOW MUCH SPENDING MONEY SHOULD I TAKE?

Even package holidays are usually based on a room-only basis. A daily budget of 350F–500F per person would not be extravagant if you are eating out three times a day and planning to buy some souvenirs.

EATING OUT

This will be your most expensive outlay, particularly if you are staying in the resort. The restaurants in the park are all similarly priced, about 30F–40F a person for a one-course self-service lunch and 150F–250F a person for a three-course table service dinner. See Chapter Seven for full details of eating out and recommended restaurants.

To give you an idea of the cost of living at Euro Disney, below are a list of items that you may want to buy there. As you will see the prices vary considerably, according to whether these are purchased in the hotels, in the theme park or in Festival Disney.

Ice-cream

- 6F for a Glace Mickey Dingo at Esso Garage (next to Hotel Santa Fe)
- 12F for one scoop of ice-cream at Fantasia Gelati (Fantasyland)
- 15F for a Mickey Bar from a stall in the theme park
- 22F for an ice-cream float from Gibson Girl Ice-Cream Parlour (Main Street USA)
- 45F for a sorbet at the Steakhouse (Festival Disney)
- 65F for a sorbet in Parkside Diner (Hotel New York)
- 65F for an ice-cream sundae at Café Fantasia (Hotel Disneyland)

Hamburgers

- 14F in Esso Garage (next to Hotel Santa Fe)
- 30F for cheeseburger and chips at Au Chalet de la Marionnette (Fantasyland)
- 42F for burger and chips at Crockett's Tavern (Camp Davy Crockett)
- 65F for a burger and chips at Annette's (Festival Disney)
- 125F for a burger with cheddar cheese and bacon at Steakhouse (Festival Disney)

Portions of Chips

- 5F from Market House Deli (Main Street USA)
- 9F 90 at Esso Garage (next to Hotel Santa Fe)
- 15F at Crockett's Tavern (Camp Davy Crockett)
- 25F at Key West (Festival Disney)
- 27F at Annette's (Festival Disney)
- 35F in a Disney hotel

Coffee

- 3F 90 in Esso Garage (next to Hotel Santa Fe)
- 5F from Casey's Corner (Main Street USA)
- 10F from Plaza Gardens (Main Street USA)
- 12F from Carnegie's (Festival Disney)
- 15F in Red Garter Saloon (Hotel Cheyenne)

Coca Cola

- 3F 90 in Esso Garage (next to Hotel Santa Fe)
- 8F in Market House Deli (Main Street USA)
- 15F in 57th Street Bar (Hotel New York)

- 15F in Billy Bob's Bar (Festival Disney)
- 16F from mini-bar (Hotel Cheyenne)

Beers

NB *Alcohol is not available in the theme park.*
- 3F 10 for can of Stella Artois at Alamo Trading Post (Camp Davy Crockett)
- 8F for a can of Kronenbourg 1664 at Esso Garage (next to Hotel Santa Fe)
- 18F for Kronenbourg in Crockett's Tavern (Camp Davy Crockett)
- 22F for Kronenbourg 1664 in mini-bar (Hotel Cheyenne)
- 24F for a Budweiser in 57th Street Bar (Hotel New York)
- 30F for a Budweiser in Billy Bob's Bar (Festival Disney)

Sandwiches

- 12F for toasted cheese sandwich at Esso Garage (next to Hotel Santa Fe)
- 25F for ham and cheese sandwich at Captain Hook's Gallery (Adventureland)
- 30F for hot pastrami, turkey or roast beef sandwich at Market House Deli (Main Street USA)
- 36F for a roast beef sandwich and chips at Toad Hall Restaurant (Fantasyland)
- 49F for a smoked salmon and cream bagel in Carnegie's (Festival Disney)
- 60F for ham and cheese sandwich room service (Newport Bay Club)
- 65F for ham and cheese sandwich at Annette's (Festival Disney)

- 95F for grilled chicken sandwich at Café Fantasia (Hotel Disneyland)
- 105F for smoked salmon and cream cheese bagel in Parkside Diner (Hotel New York)
- 125F for classic club sandwich (chicken, tomato, bacon and lettuce) in the Steakhouse (Festival Disney)

Pizzas

- 31F 50 at Pizzeria Bella Notte (Fantasyland)
- 50F–75F at Cape Cod (Newport Bay Club)
- 80F–95F at Los Angeles Bar and Grill (Festival Disney)

CHAPTER THREE

BOOKING YOUR HOLIDAY

This chapter tells you how to get to Euro Disney and the best ways to book your holiday.

How to get to Euro Disney

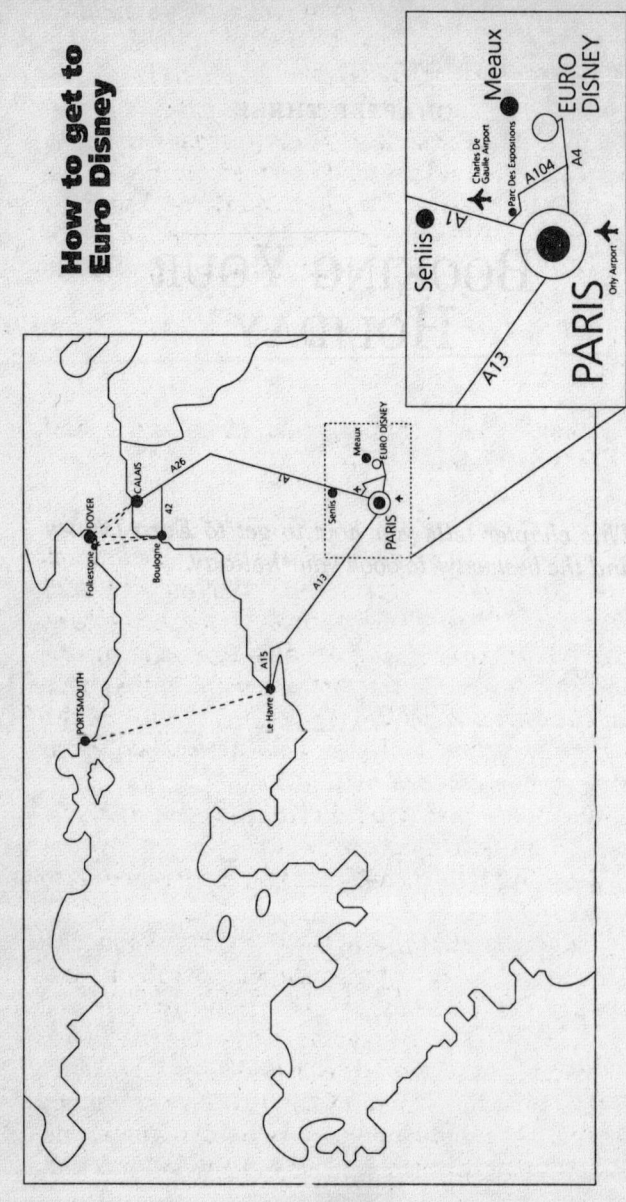

BOOKING YOUR HOLIDAY

HOW TO GET THERE

32km east of Paris, Euro Disney is easy to get to from the UK and centrally located on the A4 for France and nearby European countries. The RER train runs direct from central Paris to Euro Disney. It is also near two international airports (Charles de Gaulle and Orly).

BY CAR:

Journey Time: Approximately three and a half hours from Calais.

Euro Disney is approximately 328 km from Calais, an easy but rather boring drive along autoroutes and main roads. From Calais follow the A26 through St Omer towards Arras. From Arras, take the A1 towards Paris, turning off after Roissy-Charles de Gaulle Airport on to the A104. This will lead you on to the A4. Follow the A4 in the Reims direction and you will shortly see Euro Disney signposted on your left.

There are plenty of service stations and restaurants to stop at on this route.

It costs 84F for the tolls between Calais and Euro Disney.

AA Roadwatch has a Disney information line (Tel: 0836 401400) giving details of routes from the Channel ports and of traffic hold-ups.

Parking: Euro Disney has a huge car park with space for 11,000 cars. It costs 30F per day. Don't forget to make a note of the exact area (named after Disney characters such as Bambi, Tigger and Pinocchio) where you park or you will have to wait until thousands of cars have exited before you find yours! A moving walkway transports you to the park entrance. Disabled visitors can park next to the Disneyland Hotel. Hotel guests use the hotel car parks.

BY TRAIN:

Journey Time: Approximately three hours from Calais to Paris. Approximately 35–45 minutes from Paris to Euro Disney by RER.

You can take the train via Dover or Portsmouth to Paris and then the RER train to the entrance of Euro Disney. The RER connects Euro Disney to five Parisian stations (Etoile, Auber, Châtelet, Gare de Lyon and Nation).

In 1994 the highspeed TGV will enable you to travel direct to Euro Disney from London in three and a half hours.

BY PLANE:

Journey Time: Approximately one hour by plane from London Heathrow to Roissy-Charles de Gaulle or Orly then 30–45 minutes transfer depending on traffic. There are shuttle buses from both airports to Euro Disney charging 65F for the journey.

BY COACH:

Journey Time: Approximately four hours from Calais to Euro Disney or Paris. Several tour operators run package holidays with coach transport to Euro Disney (or to accommodation in Paris). See below.

WHEN TO GO

Euro Disney is open 365 days a year. In order to avoid the worst of the crowds, it is best not to book during the French school holidays, Easter, May 1st (Labour Day in France, Belgium and Germany) and Bastille Day (July 14th). If you are planning a short trip, mid-week is also quieter (and packages then are usually cheaper) than weekends.

MAKING YOUR RESERVATION

There are several ways to book a holiday at Euro Disney. British residents can make a hotel reservation directly with Euro Disney by phoning 071 753 2900 – you will then be connected to Euro Disney's central reservations office in Paris but charged at the UK rate.

Non-British residents can use the following numbers for booking:

33 1 49 41 49 80 (Dutch)
33 1 49 41 49 41 (French)
33 1 49 41 49 90 (German)
33 1 49 41 49 30 (Italian)
33 1 49 41 49 65 (Portuguese)
33 1 49 41 49 60 (Spanish)
33 1 49 41 49 70 (Swedish)

If you just book hotel accommodation you will then have to buy entry passes to the park from your hotel lobby (see Admission Fees below).

Alternatively, you can book a holiday with a "preferred travel partner" or a "selected tour operator". The advantage of this is that the package will include accommodation and a "Length of Stay" passport which guarantees you unlimited use of the theme park throughout your stay.

PREFERRED TRAVEL PARTNERS

British Airways and P&O European Ferries are "preferred travel partners".

British Airways Holidays (Tel: 0293 611911)
Accommodation available at all six Euro Disney Resort hotels. Holidays include scheduled flights and unlimited entry to the theme park.

P&O European Ferries Holidays (Tel: 0304 214422)
Short breaks and holidays in any of the Euro Disney hotels or Camp Davy Crockett, from two nights to a fortnight or more, by car or train. You can also buy a through ticket from Northern Ireland on P&O European Ferries Larne – Cairnryan route.

Your Disney holiday begins as soon as you board the P&O Ferry with special Euro Disney exhibitions on-board the 'Pride of Calais' and 'Pride of Dover', play areas and cartoons for children to watch.

SELECTED DISNEY TOUR OPERATORS

Airtours (Tel: 0706 26000)
Their brochure features four Euro Disney Resort

BOOKING YOUR HOLIDAY

hotels (Cheyenne, Santa Fe, Newport Bay Club, Sequoia Lodge), Camp Davy Crockett and off-site accommodation in Paris.

One week trips comprising three nights in Euro Disney and four nights in Paris (or vice versa) also available.

Cresta (Tel: 0345 056511)
Brochure features five of Euro Disney Resort hotels, as well as a wide selection of off-site accommodation both locally and in Paris. You have a choice of travelling by air, rail or self-drive.

Eurocamp/Sunsites (Tel: 0565 633844)
Specialist camping operator featuring Camp Davy Crockett.

Paris Travel Service (Tel: 0920 461000)
Accommodation available in all on-site hotels, Camp Davy Crockett and Paris. Travel by coach, rail, self-drive and chartered or scheduled air. Includes unlimited entry to the theme park and a one-day Paris Metro Pass.

Sunworld (Tel: 0532 393020)
Short breaks and long weekends to Euro Disney with accommodation available at four resort hotels, Camp Davy Crockett and in nearby hotels and Paris. Travel by air from Gatwick or Manchester.

Wallace Arnold (Tel: 0532 636456)
Accommodation available at all six resort hotels, plus Camp Davy Crockett. Travel by coach.

ASSURED ENTRY

There are almost 100 other tour operators who can include entrance tickets to Euro Disney in a package. These tour operators offer accommodation off-site, in nearby hotels or in Paris. Do check when booking that the tour operator, like those listed below, guarantees access to the resort.

Haven France & Spain (Tel: 0705 466111)
Accommodation at Campanile hotels.

Caravan & Camping Service (Tel: 071 792 1944)
Accommodation in nearby camp site, Le Pré St-Jean (*see page 60*) with guaranteed entry to Euro Disney.

Frames Rickards (Tel: 071 837 6311)
Coach tour operator offering four-day fun trips to Euro Disneyland Theme Park.

Thomsons Eurofun (Tel: 081 200 8733)
Packages with accommodation in Paris.

TRAVELLING INDEPENDENTLY

One of the cheapest ways to go to Euro Disney is to book your own accommodation off-site (*see page 50 for places to stay*). One, two or three-day passports can be bought at the main gate of Euro Disney.

Admission charges

One day 225F (150F children under 12)
Two days 425F (285F children under 12)
Three days 505F (375F children under 12)
Free entrance for children under three.

The entrance fee allows you free unlimited use of all rides and attractions, except the Rustler Roundup Shootin' Gallery. The park is open from 9am-midnight in high season, closing at 7pm in low season. All times are subject to change without notice, so check with Guest Relations (Tel: 64 74 30 00) when you arrive.

CHAPTER FOUR

WHERE TO STAY

There are three main choices of accommodation. You can either stay on-site in Disney's hotels, nearby in local accommodation, or in Paris itself. In this chapter we review Disney's hotels and also suggest some other local places to stay.

EURO DISNEY'S ACCOMMODATION

There are six Disney hotels and a campsite, designed by American and French architects. Each hotel is a themed attraction in itself, so staying there continues the Disney holiday experience.

One of the advantages of the Disney hotels is that they are all located close to the theme park, so there is no commuting and all the restaurants and entertainment are on your doorstep. If you are staying in Disney accommodation, you do not need your own car, as you can walk everywhere or use their free shuttle bus service.

The main disadvantage of Disney's accommodation is the price, which is considerably more than local hotels. However, with Disney you are guaranteed good quality, excellent facilities and polite service. The rooms are all designed to sleep four, most with two double beds, so they do work out more economical for families than for couples or single people. Be prepared, however, for smaller rooms than in the States and baths that have been designed with very short people in mind! For more space, you can book a suite. Non-smoking rooms and rooms for disabled people are also available.

One niggle about the Disney hotels is that you cannot book in until 3pm, sometimes later if your room is not ready. The cast members are trained to apologise, smile sweetly and to suggest that you leave your luggage with them and go straight off to the theme park. If you have driven all the way from the UK, this is probably the last thing you feel like doing, particularly if you have weary children in tow. From personal experience, we suggest you have a leisurely drive down to Euro

Disney, stop for lunch on the way and don't try to book in until well after 3pm.

There are six hotels of different price categories, all based on a theme of a particular American region and period, as well as a campground, Camp Davy Crockett. These are all reviewed below.

Credit Cards

All the hotels accept American Express, Eurocard, Master Card, Visa, Carte Bleue, travellers' cheques and Eurocheques.

Currencies can be exchanged at all the receptions.

The prices quoted below are for the room rate only, booked directly with Euro Disney (Tel: 071 753 2900). Booking in this way guarantees entrance to the park but does not include the cost of the passport. Theme park passports can be purchased at the information desks in the hotels. Package holidays (*see pages 30–2*) include entrance passports.

THE DISNEYLAND HOTEL

Price of rooms:
From 1,600F–1,950F per room per night; from 1,950F–12,500F per suite per night.

Overall opinion:
The best location of all the Disney hotels and very pretty.

Description:

This is the top Euro Disney hotel, styled like a candy-pink Victorian palace with a giant Mickey Mouse clockface and twinkling lights outside; and pretty pastel colours, Disney paintings and daintily carved Tinkerbells on the furniture inside.

Apart from being so pretty, the main attraction of this luxury hotel is its location, right at the entrance to the theme park, overlooking Main Street USA and the Magic Kingdom.

The hotel, which will appeal to little girls with rich daddies, was obviously not to the liking of Don Johnson and Melanie Griffith, who apparently booked out and transferred to the more sophisticated Hotel New York when they came over for the Euro Disney opening in April 1992. Because of its location, and impressive style, this will always be a popular hotel and it is already fully booked for New Year's Eve 1999!

Children's rating:

Children will love this hotel as the decor is so pretty and they are staying so near the park and their favourite characters.

Guest Rooms:

There are 500 rooms, including 21 suites, the best of which overlook the theme park. In keeping with the rest of the hotel, the rooms are decorated in pretty, pastel colours with light wood furniture and Tinkerbell carved on the wardrobes. The suites are named after Disney characters such as Bambi.

WHERE TO STAY

Facilities:
Disneyland Pool and Club offering aerobics, gym, jacuzzi, massage, sauna, solarium, steam room and indoor swimming pool. Games room. In-room babysitting service.

Eating and Drinking:
Main Street Lounge – Elegant place to sit and sip a cocktail, overlooking Main Street USA.
Café Fantasia – A fun Disney-themed café where the family can meet for a big ice-cream sundae at the end of the day.
Inventions – Buffet meals of regional American cuisine, for breakfast, lunch and dinner.
California Grill – Casual, elegant dining with Californian cuisine.

Shopping:
Galerie Mickey – Victorian-style shop selling unusual Disney memorabilia, cuddly toys etc as well as designer clothes (Lacoste, Théorème, Cacharel, Diapositive).

HOTEL NEW YORK

Price of rooms:
From 1,100F–1,600F per room per night; from 1,700F–7,200F per suite per night.

Overall opinion:
Looks better in photographs. More suitable for sophisticated couples than families.

Description:

This luxury hotel looks like a comic book cut-out, a pastiche of New York architecture, complete with Manhattan Tower, Gramercy Park Wing, brownstone buildings and a Rockefeller Centre outdoor ice-skating rink. The overall effect is dreary and the cold businesslike atmosphere is enhanced by the adjoining New York Coliseum Convention Centre.

The rust and grey interior colour scheme represents the drabber characteristics of Art Deco. There are, however, some nice design details such as the stylish Art Deco elevators and the elegant Club Manhattan restaurant, styled as the Rainbow Room in New York.

Children's rating:

Not much fun, except in winter when the outdoor ice-skating rink is open.

Guest Rooms:

574 Art Deco-themed rooms, including 36 suites. A typical room has stripey wallpaper, a Big Apple drinks cabinet (housing TV and mini-bar), a table light in the shape of the Empire State Building and New York pictures.

Facilities:

Two floodlit tennis courts. Outdoor ice-skating rink (in winter only). Hairdressers/beauty salon. Games arcade. Downtown Athletic Club featuring aerobics and gym, jacuzzi, massage, sauna, solarium, steam room and an ugly-looking swimming pool, the indoor section of which looks as

WHERE TO STAY

though it is housed in an industrial building. In-room babysitting service.

Eating and Drinking:
Club Manhattan Lounge – Elegant bar for a drink before eating in the Club Manhattan restaurant.
57th Street Bar – Laid-back place for a drink in the lobby of the hotel. Log fires make this one of the cosier areas in the hotel.
Parkside Diner – New York-style diner with huge portions and potentially huge bills (a sorbet here cost me 65F!). Good for breakfast.
Club Manhattan Restaurant – Elegant restaurant for dinner-dancing in the style of the Rainbow Room in New York. Jacket and tie required.

Shopping:
Stock Exchange – Disney memorabilia (cuddly toys etc) as well as New York souvenirs such as t-shirts and hold-alls (fun for teenagers) and designer clothes by Lacoste, Diapositive, and Daniel Cremieux.

NEWPORT BAY CLUB
(closed during winter)

Price of rooms:
From 750F–900F per room per night; from 1,000F–1,550F per suite per night.

Overall opinion:
Most elegant of all the hotels and the nautical theme works well. Recommended.

Description:

This is a very attractive hotel at the far side of Lake Buena Vista, built in the style of an elegant New England turn-of-the-century beach palace.

The nautical theme works very well with portholes in the corridor doors, cast members dressed like sailors and a giant globe in the lobby which fascinates the kids. The decor (predominantly navy, red and white) is simplistic but stylish and the yacht club atmosphere is enhanced by a harbour lighthouse and a verandah with rocking chairs overlooking the lake.

Children's rating:
Great fun, particularly for teenagers.

Guest Rooms:
This is a huge hotel with 1,098 rooms, including 15 suites. The best rooms overlook the lake. All the rooms are nautically themed with schooner-printed curtains, nautical bed heads, bold stripey wallpaper in the bathrooms, and a bright design that would delight most teenage boys.

Facilities:
The Nantucket indoor-outdoor swimming pool is particularly attractive. The health club also offers aerobics and gym, jacuzzi, massage, sauna, solarium and steam room. Croquet field. Games arcade. Children's playground with look-out tower. In-room babysitting service.

Eating and Drinking:
Fisherman's Wharf – Comfortable lounge bar off the main lobby, overlooking the lake. Cosmopolitan atmosphere with live piano music every night.
Cape Cod – Informal restaurant with an American menu of pizzas, fresh seafood and pastas. Character breakfasts (*see page 129*) served here.
The Yacht Club – More formal restaurant (jackets required) serving speciality shellfish including the New England Clambake (steamed clams, potatoes, sausages, chicken, lobster and corn on the cob).

Shopping:
Bay Boutique – Standard Disney memorabilia. Also Osh Kosh children's wear and clothing with a nautical theme.

SEQUOIA LODGE

Price of rooms:
From 750F–900F per room per night; from 1,150F–1,550F per suite per night.

Overall opinion:
The least Disneyfied hotel. Refined and relaxed rustic retreat.

Description:
You can smell the pine needles as you walk round the beautiful wooded grounds of this hotel, which has been built in the style of a lodge in the American National Parks.

The hotel looks much classier up close than it

does from across the lake. It's just a shame that the hotel has to look over to the unsightly Festival Disney!

This is a good hotel all year round – cool and refreshing in summer, warm and welcoming (log fires and lots of dark wood panelling) in winter.

The interior decor is very tasteful with flag-stoned floors, elegant framed pictures of wildlife and beautiful redwood furnishings.

Children's rating:
More of a peaceful retreat for the grown-ups.

Guest Rooms:
There are 1,011 hunting lodge-style rooms, including 14 suites. The bedrooms are decorated with rich redwood furniture, patchwork-quilt duvets and pictures of wildlife or mountain scenes.

Facilities:
Quarry Pool Health Club offering aerobics, gym, jacuzzi, massage, sauna, solarium, steam room and indoor-outdoor swimming pool. Games arcade room. Children's playground. In-room babysitting service.

Eating and Drinking:
Redwood Bar and Lounge – Lobby bar with log fire and live piano music.
Beaver Creek Tavern – American BBQ Grill with chicken, beef and rib specialities.
Hunger's Grill – Rôtisserie specialising in marinated meats.

Shopping:
Northwest Passage – Disney memorabilia and National Park theme gifts.

HOTEL CHEYENNE

Price of rooms:
From 550F–750F per room per night.

Overall opinion:
The most imaginative of all the Disney hotels. Great fun and good value for families.

Description:
This hotel is styled like a frontier town of the American West. You feel as though you are staying on a film set and that John Wayne is going to come busting out of one of the guest buildings at any moment!

The Wild West atmosphere starts from the moment you arrive. All the cast members are trained to say "Howdy" although this sounds very funny when pronounced by some of the French cast.

There is a big log fire in the large bustling reception area. Rooms are located in themed frontier guest buildings along Main Street. Children will love it here, as it is an ideal setting for playing cowboys and Indians amongst covered wagons, wigwams and teepees.

Children's rating:
Brilliant fun. They won't want to stay anywhere else!

Guest Rooms:

There are 1,000 rooms. The rooms are small but have been designed with much imagination. There are holes from gunshots in the wooden double beds and bunkbeds for the children. Other details include a wooden mini-bar with lone star motif, a lamp in the shape of a cowboy boot and curtains made out of what looks like a giant cowboy's scarf. There is even buffalo printed carpet!

Facilities:

Fort Apache playground and Indian Village for the children. Yellow Rose Dance Hall. Arcade games room. In-room babysitting service.

Eating:

Red Garter Saloon – Cosy Wild West saloon bar with log fire and live country music in the evenings.

Chuck Wagon Café – Large self-service restaurant with pioneer-style dishes which you select from specialist wagons such as the Range Rider Barbecue Pit, Cowgirls' Salad Wagon and the Last Chance Watering Hole. One of the best value places to eat in Euro Disney. Breakfast is superb, with steaming porridge served out of cowboy bowls, giant plates of berries and fresh fruit, pancakes with maple syrup and other cooked dishes. Also good for dinner – 89F for a huge plate of barbecued food.

Shopping:

General Store – Disney memorabilia and western theme goods.

HOTEL SANTA FE

Price of rooms:
From 450F–550F per room per night.

Overall opinion:
Not recommended. Cheap and tacky-looking.

Description:
Styled on the American South-West, this is the least inspiring of all the Disney accommodation with barren-looking New Mexico desert surrounds, dusty-looking buildings and an incredibly tacky billboard poster of Clint Eastwood at the entrance.

The reception area is characterless and uninviting. It is the sort of hotel you would expect to find on a cheap package holiday to the Canary Islands.

Children's rating:
They will prefer to stay at the Cheyenne on the other side of the Rio Grande river.

Guest Rooms:
There are 1,000 Santa Fe-style rooms in 42 pueblos. The decor in the rooms is bright and cheerful with Aztec-style patchwork bedspreads.

Facilities:
Totem Circle Playground. Pow Wow games arcade room. In-room babysitting service.

Eating and Drinking:
Rio Grande Bar – Serving cocktails such as José's Pick Up, Tequila Sunrise, Howling Coyote and Sombrero. Live music in the evenings.
La Cantina – Self-service style restaurant offering a variety of American Tex-Mex specialities such as black bean soup and chilli con carne.

Shopping:
Trading Post – Small shop selling Disney memorabilia and cheap-looking New Mexico theme goods.

CAMP DAVY CROCKETT

Price of cabins:
575F–875F per night (sleeps six). Tents 270F.

Overall opinion:
Great fun for families; relaxing wooded location.

Description:
You realise that this is no ordinary campsite when you drive in under the entrance and see Mickey Mouse dressed up as Davy Crockett on the nameplate.

Children will love this wooded campsite, about 10 km away from Euro Disney, designed in early American pioneer style with a western fort and log cabins. The latter are actually just mobile homes decked in wood, but they are extremely spacious and luxurious, each with a dishwasher, microwave, colour television, telephone, outdoor picnic table and barbecue. There is one bedroom with a double bed and bunk beds and another pull-out double bed in the lounge. Bathrooms are small but the baths themselves are actually bigger than in the Disney hotels.

One of the main financial advantages of staying in this campsite is that you can self-cater. The village store stocks food although it is more economical to come with a well-stocked car or drive out to a local supermarket for provisions.

The log cabins are grouped in fairly close proximity – with everyone's car parked outside their home it actually looks very suburban. You wake up in the morning, however, to the sound of the birds singing and the overall atmosphere is very relaxing.

Apart from the 414 cabins, there are also 181 campsites, each with water, washing facilities, electrical hook-ups and a picnic table.

It is a shame that the village (where you will find Crockett's Tavern, Davy's Farm, Blue Springs Pool and tennis courts) is located so close to the motorway as the roar of passing vehicles spoils the illusion of a wilderness retreat.

Children's rating:
They'll love it! The superb facilities for children (see below) mean that you could easily spend a couple of days in the camp without venturing out to Euro Disney.

Facilities:
Davy's Farm – A chance for little children to stroke their favourite farmyard animals and go on pony rides. Bicycle rentals – a healthy way to travel round the camp. Nature, bike and jogging

trails. Sports fields, tennis courts, campfire, children's playgrounds.

Blue Springs Pool – Beautiful indoor swimming complex next to the restaurant with slides, river waterfall, spa and health food bar. Modest swimmers may feel self-conscious that the changing rooms are communal although you can change in your own cubicle! My only criticism is that it is not very hygienic walking through the changing rooms to the pool in outdoor shoes.

Eating and Drinking:

Crockett's Tavern – Small, bright bar and self-service restaurant serving excellent hamburgers and other family fare. Part of the attractive pine building houses Blue Springs Pool so you can watch the swimmers while you eat.

Shopping:

Alamo Trading Post – Disney memorabilia plus food and drink. More expensive than a local supermarket.

WHERE TO STAY OUTSIDE EURO DISNEY

The main advantage of staying outside Euro Disney is the cost, particularly if you are a couple or a single person, unwilling to utilise the "rooms for four" basis on which the Disney hotels operate.

Another advantage is that it gives you the opportunity to explore the local countryside and sample the flavour of the real France. Staying in Euro Disney, it is easy to forget you are in France at all.

You can book accommodation independently or

through a tour operator (*see page 30*). If you book independently, remember that you will have to pay to get into the park.

MOTELS

The nearest accommodation to Euro Disney is in modern and rather uninspiring satellite towns. Here you will find plenty of cheap motel-type establishments (from about 140F–350F per night). The rooms are basic but comfortable and the motels usually have a cheap restaurant to eat in.

Most of the places below can cater for children in your room, either free or for a minimal charge. Motels, such as the Campanile range, offer good facilities for disabled people.

Although this type of accommodation will not give you much insight into French culture (motels are motels, whichever country you are in), they are perfectly adequate for a night or two, and after a long day touring round Euro Disney you will probably just want to go to bed.

Below are some of the best motels in the vicinity. Prices are for the room per night, not per person.

LES RELAIS BLEUS
St Thibault-des-Vignes (Tel: 64 02 02 44)
Distance from Euro Disney: 11 km.
Small, clean, bright motel with a more intimate atmosphere than some of the bigger local establishments. Communal parts are very well kept and rooms are small but adequate for a night or two. The food in the restaurant is very good – more imaginative than just steak and chips but not too

gourmet to cater for the whole family's tastes. 78F menu (45F children's menu).
320F per night (405F for a room with three beds).

BALLADINS HOTEL
Torcy (Tel: 60 17 63 09)
Distance from Euro Disney: 10km.
Cheap, modern hotel with free bed in your room for under-twelves. Television available at an extra 24F per night.
189F per night.

HOTEL 1 PREMIERE CLASS
Torcy (Tel: 64 62 46 00)
Distance from Euro Disney: 10km.
Part of the Hotel Campanile complex in Torcy (see below). Rooms comprise a double bed, a single bunk-bed with shower, wash-basin, toilet and TV. Cold and hot beverages and toiletry articles are available from vending machines. You can eat cheaply at the Campanile hotel opposite or at the Côte à Côte restaurant next door. 18F breakfast.
139F per night.

RESTHOTEL PRIMEVERE
Meaux Beauval (Tel: 64 33 88 11)
Distance from Euro Disney: 16km.
A good hotel for families. Located next door to the Place Beauval shopping complex. Prettier than average bedrooms, all with telephone, satellite TV and private bathroom. Cots can be provided. Two disabled rooms. Tiled restaurant with 76F buffet menu. Breakfast 30F.
260F per night.

HOTEL CAMPANILE
Torcy (Tel: 60 17 84 85)
Distance from Euro Disney: 10km.
Part of a high-quality chain of French hotels providing comfortable motel-style accommodation. This is the nearest Campanile hotel to Euro Disney. It has a 24-hour reception, plenty of parking space and a cheap restaurant that serves dinner (83F menu includes three courses and wine) until 10pm every night. Children's menu 39F for four courses and a drink. Rooms are clean, functional and easy to get to from your car. It is a good hotel for disabled people (well-designed handicapped rooms). All rooms have TV, radio alarm, telephone and private bathroom.

If you stay here it is a good idea to prepare yourself for a long day at Euro Disney at their "all you can eat" buffet breakfast.
330F per room per night.

HOTEL CAMPANILE
Meaux (Tel: 60 23 41 41)
Distance from Euro Disney: 17km.
Part of the same chain as the Campanile in Torcy with a cheap restaurant and similar facilities. The advantage of staying in this one is that it is only a few minutes from the centre of Meaux, an interesting old town to explore and shop in (*see pages 216–9*).
Room prices are also cheaper.
258F per night.

HOTEL MERCURE
Saint-Witz, Fosses (Tel: 34 68 28 28 or book through their London office 071 724 1000)
Another big chain of French hotels and a good place to stay if you plan to visit Parc Asterix (two

minutes away) as well as Euro Disney (20–30 minutes drive). Don't be put off by the cheap-looking exterior. It actually looks much nicer inside. The hotel has an attractive bar area and restaurant, and 115 rooms, all with bathrooms, TV, telephone and mini-bar. Under-16s can share parents' room for free. Children's menu and bargain breakfast available.
From 315F per room per night.

HOTEL ACOSTEL
Meaux (Tel: 64 33 28 58)
Distance from Euro Disney: 17km.
Although this motel-style hotel looks rather shabby from the road, it is actually a good place to stay, particularly in summer. The staff are friendly and the clean, comfortable bedrooms open out on to the swimming pool and overlook the River Marne. There is no hotel restaurant (although they do serve breakfast) but you will find plenty of places to eat nearby.
275F per night.

HOTEL CLIMAT
Meaux (Tel: 64 33 83 80)
Distance from Euro Disney: 18km.
This is a fairly typical local motel with 60 clean, simply decorated bedrooms. There are also rooms for disabled people. Its main feature is La Soupière, its restaurant, located in a separate building with an aviary of exotic birds. Menu 80F (40F for children). Breakfast 30F.
260F per night (extra 25F for a room with a television).

AUBERGES

If you are looking for somewhere more traditional to stay there are several small family-run auberges in the local vicinity. These are usually more suitable for couples than families as the rooms have not always been updated to cater for more than two.

One of the main advantages of staying in an auberge is that they often have excellent restaurants with gourmet menus, fitting in with the French principle that eating is always more important than sleeping!

Below are some of the best auberges and traditional accommodation nearby.

LE PLAT D'ETAIN
Jouarre (Tel: 60 22 06 07)
Distance from Euro Disney: 28 km.
It is a short drive (about 20 minutes) along the autoroute from the old village of Jouarre to Euro Disney. If you are looking for somewhere traditional to stay, this small auberge (part of the Logis de France chain) is ideal with 24 well-maintained bedrooms and an exceptionally pretty dining-room with a beamed ceiling and carved wooden chairs. Jouarre itself is a working market town. The auberge is a few metres away from the market where locals barter for chickens, rabbits, lambs and other livestock. There is also an old abbey to visit a couple of minutes walk away.

The auberge is more suitable for couples than families.

AUBERGE LE SOUTERRAIN
Crecy-la-Chapelle (Tel: 64 36 92 15)
Distance from Euro Disney: 8 km.
This small roadside auberge is full of character and charm, with 15 old-fashioned rooms. Downstairs is all dark wood and lace, and local painters (including Corot) have left murals as way of payment for their board and lodging. Pretty restaurant and walled garden for summer dining. More suitable for couples or single travellers than families. The nearby village of Crecy-la-Chapelle is one of the prettiest and most traditional in the Euro Disney vicinity. Ask for a room at the back of the building as the auberge is located by a busy road.
290F for a room per night. Half-board 255F per person (good value if you plan to come back to the hotel to eat at night).

HOSTELLERIE LE GONFALON
Germigny L'Evèque (Tel: 64 33 16 05)
Distance from Euro Disney: 22 km.
If you want a pretty, romantic little place to stay with a superb restaurant, this hostellerie is ideal. This friendly family-run hotel is set overlooking the Marne river in a sleepy little village a few minutes drive away from Meaux. There are only ten bedrooms, the best of which have balconies overlooking the river. Rooms at the top of the house are small. The elegant restaurant (a popular place with locals) is superb, and as you will guess from the big lobster tank, specialises in seafood and gourmet food. Expect to pay double the room rate for dîner-à-deux.
280F–320F per night.

HOTEL LE PRIEURE
Ermenonville (Tel: 44 54 00 44)
Distance from Euro Disney: 22km.
Ermenonville is one of the older, more attractive villages near Euro Disney. The Priory (le Prieure) is a beautiful old building in the heart of the village, next to the church. The interior is beautifully furnished with period pieces. Monsieur and Madame Treillou run the place with great pride as if it were their own home. There are ten bedrooms, the best being located on the first floor. Rooms at the top are hot and stuffy on summer nights. Although it is a beautiful hotel, it is not a place for peace and quiet. Some of the rooms overlook a busy road, others look on to the church which chimes all night, every hour! Ask for a room on the other side of the house. There is no restaurant but there are several places to eat in the village.
450F per night with shower, 500F with bath.

AUBERGE DU PETIT CHEVAL D'OR
Plailly (Tel: 44 54 36 33)
Distance from Euro Disney: 25 km.
This charming roadside auberge near Ermenonville is only a few minutes from Parc Asterix and a pleasant 20–30 minutes drive from Euro Disney. There are 21 rooms, all with television, 16 with bathrooms and five with showers.
From 180F to 320F per night.

HOSTELLERIE DU COUNTRY-CLUB
Samois-sur-Seine, near Fontainebleau
(Tel: 64 24 60 34)
Distance from Euro Disney: 65km.
Although it is too far to commute to Euro Disney

every day, this is a charming riverside place to stay if you want to extend your holiday with a day or two in the Fontainebleau area (*see Chapter Eleven: Excursions*). Located about 9km from the hustle and bustle of Fontainebleau, Samois-sur-Seine is a quiet, pretty village full of beautiful villas, fashionable restaurants and flower-decked bridges for romantic walks. The hotel has a terrace overlooking the river for sunbathing and summer dining and a tennis court. The rooms are small but comfortable, the staff welcoming.
320F per night.

CHATEAUX

If you don't mind a slightly longer drive to Euro Disney, there are several more luxurious places to stay in converted châteaux. These usually have exceptionally good restaurants and are a good base for exploring the local countryside. Below are some suggestions.

HOSTELLERIE DU CHATEAU
(*Tel: 23 82 21 13*)
Distance from Euro Disney: 90km.
For the ultimate in luxury, stay at this beautiful château in the Champagne region and be transported to Euro Disney by a 10-minute helicopter ride! The château dates back to 1206 and the ruins of the original château, built by Robert de Dreux, grandson of Louis VI, are preserved in the grounds of the Hostellerie. Lit up at night, it makes a very romantic setting.

Families of four are automatically upgraded to a suite. The suite in the castle turret is a splendid apartment complete with huge living area and central jacuzzi bath! Dinner in the Hostellerie is a truly gourmet experience and one to be savoured at leisure.

In conjunction with Moët & Chandon, the Hostellerie is organising special Euro Disney breaks which include entrance tickets to the theme park and a Champagne tour and tasting. This works out at very good value – from 590F per person for one night in a suite, including breakfast, entry into Euro Disney, a presentation box of champagne, and a visit to the Moët & Chandon cellars nearby. An additional night at the Hostellerie with a two-day Euro Disney pass is available at 517F supplement. Helicopter transfers are at extra cost. If you want a treat, stay here!

CHATEAU DE GRAND ROMAINE
Lesigny (Tel: 60 02 21 24)
Distance from Euro Disney: 22 km.
Set in 70 acres of parkland, this château hotel has 90 rooms which are separate from the original château. Leisure facilities include two outdoor swimming pools, five tennis courts, volleyball, golf practice nets, table tennis, sauna and games rooms. Golf courses available nearby. Panoramic views from restaurant.
520F per night.

CHATEAU MORTEFONTAINE
Plailly (Tel: 44 54 30 94 or through London booking agency – Alliance UK 081 392 1838)
Distance from Euro Disney: 30km.
This handsome château is a little shabby at the edges, but conveniently located for Parc Asterix,

and about 30 minutes drive from Euro Disney. The best bedrooms are on the first floor – the ones above are rather cramped. The staff are all very friendly and speak English. There are large uncultivated grounds at the back of this château which date back to the seventh and eighth century. Breakfast is served in the conservatory, lunch (in summer) on the terrace, and dinner (superb, nouvelle-cuisine style) in a small, panelled dining-room. 45F continental breakfast, 60F buffet breakfast.
From 410F per night.

CAMPING AND CARAVANNING

Apart from Disney's luxurious Camp Davy Crockett (*see above*) there are several campsites near the theme park. Expect to pay about 50F per night at these local sites.

To book a package with ferry crossings and insurance contact Caravan & Camping Service in London (Tel: 071 792 1944).

PARC DE LA COLLINE
Torcy (Tel: 60 05 42 32)
Distance from Euro Disney: 10km.
It is a shame that this site is located near a busy road as it has good access to the sporting facilities across the road at Parc de Loisirs (*see Chapter Twelve: Excursions*). They also have chalets for rent.

PARC PRE SAINT JEAN
Crecy-la-Chapelle (Bookings through
Caravan & Camping Service in London. Tel:
071 792 1944)
Distance from Euro Disney: 15km
Simple, pretty site with a children's playground

and toilets. All other services and facilities are located in the charming old village of Crecy-la-Chapelle. Camping & Caravanning Service are selling Disney packages, including passes to Euro Disney and camping accommodation at this site.

CAMP DE LA BASE DE LOISIRS DE JABLINES
(Tel: 60 26 04 31)
Distance from Euro Disney: 12km.
Small site near Euro Disney with access to leisure facilities such as bicycle hire, waterslide and golf practice.

LES BONDONS
La Ferte-sous-Jouarre (Tel: 60 22 00 23)
Distance from Euro Disney: 28km.
Easy access to Euro Disney on A4. Quiet site in grounds of château. Caravans only.

BASE DE PLEIN-AIR
Samois-sur-Seine (Tel: 64 24 63 45)
Distance from Euro Disney: 65km.
Too far to commute to Euro Disney daily, but pretty village and centre for exploring Fontainebleau as an extension to your Disney holiday.

STAYING IN PARIS

Euro Disney is within easy reach of Paris and many tour operators are combining accommodation in the French capital with day trips to Euro Disney.

The RER train network connects Euro Disney

to five Parisian stations (Etoile, Auber, Châtelet, Gare de Lyon and Nation). The journey takes about 35 minutes from Châtelet-Les Halles.

Accommodation in Paris can be booked independently or as part of a Euro Disney package (*see page 30–2*). If you book independently, remember that you will have to pay entrance fees into the park each day.

HOTELS
There are thousands of hotels in Paris where you will pay from about 200F per night upwards. For a small fee the Paris Tourist Office (Central Welcome Service, 127 Avenue des Champs-Elysées; Tel: 47 23 61 72) can make same-day reservations for you.

SELF-CATERING
Rothray (Tel: 48 87 13 37)
Parisian apartment rental service. Seven-day minimum. All apartments are centrally located.

CAMPING AND CARAVANNING
Camping d'Île de France, Bois de Boulogne (Tel: 45 24 30 00)
The only major campsite in the Paris area. Unfortunately, you cannot make advance bookings and there are huge queues every morning in the summer – if you want a space, make sure you get there early.

CHAPTER FIVE

THE LAYOUT OF EURO DISNEY

In order to make the most of your visit, it is important to familiarise yourself with the layout of the park before you go (see map). This chapter includes brief descriptions of the five themed lands and lists everything they have to offer, including services such as stroller rental and lost property. We have highlighted (*) particularly interesting attractions in each land.

For detailed reviews of rides and attractions, see Chapter Six, for restaurants Chapter Seven, shops Chapter Eight, entertainment Chapter Nine. For suggested tours, see Chapter Ten.

Euro Disney and Resort Complex

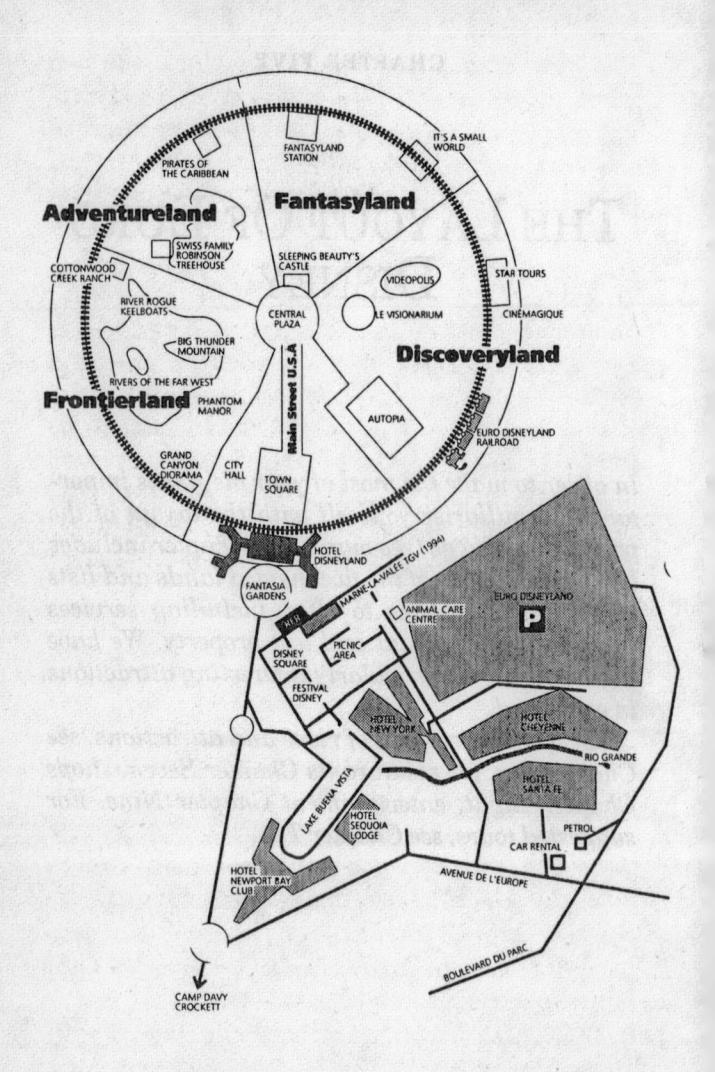

EURO DISNEY

THE LAYOUT OF EURO DISNEY

FIVE MAGICAL LANDS

The Euro Disney theme park is divided into five lands, all with distinctive architecture, landscaping, shops and restaurants. The best way to explore these are by foot, although you can also ride round aboard the steam-run Euro Disneyland Railroad.

ENTERING THE MAGIC KINGDOM

The entrance to the Magic Kingdom is truly spectacular with beautifully manicured gardens and fronted by the fairytale-looking, candy-pink Hotel Disneyland. This is the first Disney hotel to be located inside a theme park, and if you can afford a top-rate room, you can have the unforgettable pleasure of flinging back the curtains in the morning and looking straight out on to Main Street and Sleeping Beauty's Castle.

THROUGH THE TURNSTILES

As you approach the electronic turnstile gates, you are greeted by cast members asking if you already have an entrance ticket. If not, you can buy one, two or three-day passports at a booth. To avoid the queues, make sure you get there early (before 9 am). If you already have a ticket, you can go straight through into the park.

Remember that if you exit in the day, you need to get your hand stamped for re-entry.

If you need to change money, there are change kiosks located just before the ticket booths.

Other facilities outside the gates include Guest

Storage and Guest Relations (general information kiosk).

MAIN STREET USA

Best land for:

- Shopping
- Architectural detail
- Tea and cakes
- Entertainment

Your visit to Euro Disney will inevitably start in Main Street USA. This is one of the most aesthetically pleasing parts of the park, a pollution-free Utopia where the walls of the pretty, candy-coloured painted buildings are never graffitied and the pavements are spotlessly clean.

Main Street takes you back to turn of the century small-town America and is a hubbub of activity, with individually designed traditional shops and the smells of home-baked cookies and old-fashioned eating establishments.

The architectural detail is tremendous. Make sure you look up at the buildings as you walk down the street. Above Main Street Motors, for example, you can actually see the coffee cup steaming in the old Nescafé poster!

Services in Main Street USA

Babycare Centre

Next to Plaza Gardens Restaurant at the Central Plaza end of Main Street. Facilities for preparing formulas, warming bottles, breast-feeding and changing nappies. Disposable nappies and limited selection of baby food are available.

Camera Rentals
Town Square Photography, Main Street USA. Cameras and videos for hire.

City Hall
Information centre and place to pick up maps and entertainment timetables.

First Aid *(Tel: 64 74 23 00)*
Next to Plaza Gardens Restaurant on Central Plaza.

Foreign Currency
Information Booth, Main Street Station.

Lost and Found
City Hall, Main Street USA (Tel 64 74 25 00).

Lost Children
City Hall, Main Street USA or Lost Children Office next to Plaza Gardens Restaurant at the Central Plaza end of Main Street.

Lockers
Underneath the station. Operated by a 10F piece. Big enough to store handbags or small parcels.

Photo Processing
Town Square Photography, Main Street USA. Very expensive. Wait until you get home!

Strollers and Wheelchairs
Town Square Terrace. 30F plus 20F refundable deposit. You will be doing a lot of walking during the day so it is definitely worth hiring a pushchair

even for slightly older children (three or four years old) who will quickly tire themselves out by all the excitement.

Rides
Euro Disneyland Railroad★
Main Street Vehicles

Shops
Plaza West Boutique
Plaza East Boutique
The Storybook Store★
Ribbons & Bows Hat Shop
Emporium
Town Square Photography
Silhouette Artist
Boardwalk Candy Palace
Disney Clothiers, Ltd
Harrington's Fine China & Porcelains★
Disneyana Collectibles
Disney & Co
Glass Fantasies
Main Street Vehicles

Eating and drinking

Table-Service
Walt's★

Self-Service
Plaza Gardens Restaurant★

Fast-Food
Victoria's Home-Style Cooking★
Casey's Corner★
Market House Deli

Snacks and Refreshments
The Ice-Cream Company
The Coffee Grinder
Cookie Kitchen
Cable Car Bake Shop
The Gibson Girl Ice-Cream Parlour
The Bagel Cart

Entertainment
The Euro Disneyland Band
The Disney Parade★
Electrical Parade★
Also street entertainers such as:
Keystone Kops and The Barber Shop Quartet★

FRONTIERLAND

Best land for:

- Sitting in the sun and soaking up the Wild West atmosphere
- Playing cowboys and Indians

Frontierland brings to life the legends of the American frontier with a landscape inspired by Monument Valley, Utah and the Gold Rush. This is the best land to be in on a sunny day as there are all sorts of trips on Rivers of the Wild West and there is lots to watch if you just want to sit down and relax.

Rides and Attractions
Mark Twain or Molly Brown Steamboats
Phantom Manor★
Rustler Roundup Shootin' Gallery

Big Thunder Mountain Railroad★
River Rogue Keelboats
Indian Canoes
Cottonwood Creek Ranch

Shops
Tobias Norton & Sons★
Bonanza Outfitters★
Eureka Mining Supplies
Pueblo Trading Post
Woodcarver's Workshop

Eating and Drinking

Table-Service
Silver Spur Steakhouse
The Lucky Nugget Saloon★

Fast-Food
Last Chance Café
Fuente del Oro
Cowboy Cookout Barbeque★

Snacks
Railroad Spike Potatoes Cart★

Entertainment
Lucky Nugget Revue★
Gunfighters' Stunt Show★

ADVENTURELAND

Best land for:

- Exotic atmosphere at night
- Young explorers

This is the most exotic land with an exquisitely designed eastern bazaar, and a tropical island which children will love to explore. Make sure you wander round this land at night, when the torchlights and Moroccan-style buildings are tremendously atmospheric.

Rides and attractions
Adventure Isle★
Swiss Family Robinson Treehouse★
Pirates of the Caribbean★

Shops
Trader Sam's Jungle Boutique
Adventureland Bazaar –
– Le Chant des Tam-Tams
– Les Trésors de Schéhérazade
– La Reine des Serpents
– L'Echoppe d'Aladin
– La Girafe Curieuse
– Le Coffre du Capitaine★

Eating and Drinking

Table-Service
Explorer's Club★
Blue Lagoon Restaurant★

Fast-Food
Aux Épices Enchantées*

Snacks and Refreshments
Café de la Brousse
Captain Hook's Galley
Character Sandwiches Cart

Stir Fry Cart
Smoothie Cart
Barbecue Cart

Entertainment
Tam-Tams Africains
Dr Livingstone

FANTASYLAND

Best land for:

- Little children
- Fairground-style rides

Fantasyland is the prettiest and most magical land at Euro Disney. If you are travelling with young children, you will want to spend most of your time here. The highlight of Fantasyland and Euro Disney is the stunningly ornate Sleeping Beauty's Castle.

Rides and Attractions
Sleeping Beauty's Castle★
Snow White and the Seven Dwarfs
Pinocchio's Adventures
Lancelot's Carousel
Peter Pan's Flight★
Dumbo the Flying Elephant
Mad Hatter's Teacups
Alice's Curious Labyrinth
It's A Small World★

Shops
La Boutique du Château
Merlin L'Enchanteur

La Confiserie des Trois Fées
La Chaumière des Sept Nains
Sir Mickey's
La Bottega di Geppetto

Eating and Drinking

Table-Service
Auberge de Cendrillon

Fast-Food
Pizzeria Bella Notte★
Au Châlet de la Marionnette
Toad Hall Restaurant

Snacks and Refreshments
Fantasia Gelati
March Hare Refreshments
The Old Mill
Pretzel Cart
Chocolate & Caramel Fruit Cart
Pancake Griddle
Snow Ball Cart
Beverage Cart

Entertainment
C'est Magique (Fantasy Festival Stage)★
Sleeping Beauty (Le Théàtre du Château)

DISCOVERYLAND

Best land for:

- Teenagers

This land is the smallest and least impressive of

the Magical Kingdom lands, although it will appeal to teenagers and it does have the superb Star Tours ride. The futuristic architecture is designed in the way which European inventors such as Jules Verne and Leonardo da Vinci would have envisaged.

Rides and Attractions
Le Visionarium★
Orbitron
Autopia
Star Tours★
Captain EO (CinéMagique)★

Shops
Constellations
Star Traders★

Eating & Drinking

Fast-Food
Café des Visionnaires
Café Hyperion★

Snacks
Sausage Cart
Doughnut Cart

Entertainment
Road Show (Videopolis)

FESTIVAL DISNEY

Festival Disney is the entertainment centre, a few minutes walk from the park. The most attractive

THE LAYOUT OF EURO DISNEY

part of it is its location on the edge of Lake Buena Vista. Otherwise it is rather a dreary uninspiring place.

Below is a list of its facilities. For reviews of restaurants see pages 145–7, shops pages 163–5 and entertainment pages 177–8.

Services
Post Office
Boat Rental
Never Land Club (entertainment babysitting service for children)★
Tourist Office
Arcade

Shops
The Disney Store
Team Mickey
Hollywood Pictures
Surf Shop
Buffalo Trading Company
Streets of America Shop

Eating and Drinking

Table-Service
Annette's Diner
Carnegie's★
Los Angeles Bar & Grill
Key West Seafood★
The Steakhouse

Bars
Champions Sports Bar★
Billy Bob's Country and Western Saloon

Entertainment
Buffalo Bill's Wild West Show★
Hurricane's Disco
Billy Bob's Country and Western Saloon

INFORMATION DIRECTORY

Baby Care Centre
Changing tables and bottle warmers available next to Plaza Gardens Restaurant, Main Street USA.

Babysitting
Available in all the hotels and in the Never Land Club (Festival Disney).

Boat Rental
Boats can be hired outside the Steakhouse (Festival Disney).

Camera Rentals
Still and video cameras for rent at Town Square.

Car Rental
Europcar have an office near the Hotel Santa Fe, and car hire can be booked through the hotels.

Cash Machines
In Liberty Arcade and Discovery Arcade (Main Street USA).

Children's Pushchairs
Can be rented at Town Square Terrace in Main Street USA.

THE LAYOUT OF EURO DISNEY

Currency Exchange
At the Main Entrance, Main Street Station, Frontierland Depot and in Adventureland and Fantasyland. Money can also be changed in the hotels and at the Post Office.

Disabled Facilities
Special Services Guide available at City Hall (Main Street USA).

First Aid
Next to Plaza Gardens Restaurant (Main Street USA).

Lockers
Coin-operated lockers at Main Street Station. Larger items can be stored at Guest Storage, located outside the Main Entrance.

Lost Child
Report to City Hall or Lost Children next to Plaza Gardens Restaurant in Main Street USA.

Lost and Found
At City Hall in Main Street USA.

Pets
Not allowed in the park (apart from guide dogs). Pets may be left at the Animal Care Centre near the car park.

Picnic Area
Located between the car park and Disney Square. You are not allowed to bring food and beverages into the park.

Postboxes
Postboxes are located throughout the park.

Post Office
Festival Disney.

Sporting Facilities
18-hole golf course due to open in 1993 (details from City Hall). Tennis courts at Hotel New York and Camp Davy Crockett. Swimming pools at Disneyland Hotel, Hotel New York, the Newport Bay Club, the Sequoia Lodge and Camp Davy Crockett. Skating at Hotel New York. Croquet at Newport Bay Club. Health clubs at Disneyland Hotel, Hotel New York, Newport Bay Club and Sequoia Lodge. Cycling, jogging and pony rides at Camp Davy Crockett.

Telephones
Public telephones are available throughout the park.

Tourist Office
Local tourist office in Festival Disney.

Wheelchairs
Can be rented at Town Square Terrace in Main Street USA.

CHAPTER SIX

REVIEWS OF RIDES AND ATTRACTIONS

So you are finally at Euro Disney and cannot wait to try out all the rides! In this chapter we review every ride and attraction in the theme park. These are arranged under the various lands.

We have given every ride a star rating (* to *****) so that you can make an instant decision about whether you want to do this one or not. As some of the rides may be superb fun for older children but terrifying for little ones, we have indicated age suitability in our reviews. We have also included details about the best time of day to do the ride and an estimated queuing time, although bear in mind that this will vary according to the time of year (see page 29 – when to go). Rides are suitable for disabled people and pregnant women, unless stated otherwise.

After reading this chapter, you will have a good idea about which rides you want to do most. If your time at Euro Disney is limited (one or two days) we suggest you turn to Chapter Ten and follow one of our suggested itineraries. These tours have been specially designed to help you avoid the queues and see the best parts of the park.

Unfortunately, the weather in Euro Disney is not reliable. If it is a particularly wet or windy day, turn to page 210 for tips on how to cope.

The park has been reviewed in a clockwise direction, starting in Main Street USA.

MAIN STREET, USA

EURO DISNEY RAILROAD

Location: Main Street USA

Overall comment:
A fun and restful way to see the whole park. A tame ride that is well worth doing.

Ratings:
Adults: ***
Teenagers: ***
7–12 year olds: ****
4–7 year olds: *****
Toddlers: ****

Description:
This is the first ride you see in Euro Disney, a steam train that chugs its way round the 2.2km perimeter of the park, at a slow, leisurely pace.

Like everything at Disney, the attention to detail is superb. Old-fashioned prams and leather luggage wait to be "boarded" and platform

REVIEWS OF RIDES AND ATTRACTIONS

announcements warn you that shooting buffalo from the train is strictly prohibited! There are three trains, all reproduced from a late 19th-century design.

The 20-minute journey is an excellent way to acquaint yourself with the size and general layout of the park, although your view is somewhat restricted, particularly at night.

The train chugs to a halt twice, once at Frontierland and again at Fantasyland. It is more than just a train ride as you pass through a superb depiction of the Grand Canyon complete with wild cats frolicking in the sun and a wolf howling from a jagged peak. You also enter a grotto world full of skeletons and buried treasures – this might be too scary for little children if the train wasn't playing such jolly music.

Make sure you wrap up warmly, particularly if you ride the train at night. As the sides of the train are open, keep a close eye on excitable toddlers.

The train runs every 15–20 minutes. Don't make the mistake of thinking you have to use the train to get around the park, as Euro Disney is much smaller than it first appears and, if queues are long, it is quicker to walk.

Duration of ride:
20 minutes

Length of queues:
Up to 45 minutes. If the queues extend on to the street, come back later or board the train at Fantasyland or Frontierland.

Entertainment during queuing:
Funny comments of stationmaster. The 19th-century style station platform is a good vantage point to look down on everything happening on Main Street.

Best times of day to go there:
First thing in the morning as a way of getting your bearings.
Last ride of the day as a final memory of the park.

Visual and audio effects:
Fun, especially the Grand Canyon Diorama. Commentary in English, French, German and Italian.

Worth another ride?
Yes, this is a good ride to do again at the end of your visit.

MAIN STREET VEHICLES

Location: Main Street USA

Overall comment:
Various types of old-fashioned transport taking you from Town Square to Central Plaza.

Ratings:
Adults: *
Teenagers: *
7–12 year olds: **
4–7 year olds: ****
Toddlers: ****

REVIEWS OF RIDES AND ATTRACTIONS

Description:
There are all sorts of old-fashioned vehicles which will transport you down Main Street USA. These include a horse-drawn streetcar, a fire truck, a limousine and an old-fashioned paddy wagon. They are all fun for little children and good for tired feet, although not worth queuing for. For a good view of the street, jump aboard the double-decker Omnibus and enjoy the detailed façades of the buildings.

Duration of ride:
Varies.

Length of queues:
Usually minimal.

Entertainment during queuing:
Watching everything that is going on in Town Square. There is often a brass band playing in the middle and Disney characters milling around.

Best times of day to go there:
Anytime.

Worth another ride?
No.

FRONTIERLAND

BIG THUNDER MOUNTAIN RAILROAD

Location: Frontierland
Overall comment:
The best "thrill" ride in Euro Disney, with added

special effects, offering superb views of Frontierland – if you've got your eyes open!

Ratings:
Adults: *****
Teenagers: *****
For 7–12 years old: *****
4–7s: *** Only for the bolder and older children in this group. There is a height restriction.
Toddlers: Not suitable.

Also not suitable for pregnant women or anyone with back, neck or muscular problems.

Description:
All aboard the runaway mine train on this wild roller-coaster ride. Although the ride is quite tame by fairground standards, you'll still get a lurching stomach in the first few hair-raising seconds. The Wild West landscape is superbly detailed with animatronic asses, a goat which tugs the jeans from a miner's washing line and a howling coyote. Be prepared to be splashed (but not soaked) when the train plunges through water.

Duration of ride:
Three minutes.

Length of queues:
This is one of the most popular rides in Euro Disney. You may have to queue for over an hour and a half at peak times. To avoid this, do the ride as soon as you get through the gates. Not one to queue for on a rainy day as only about 15 minutes of queuing is under cover. Adults will not mind

REVIEWS OF RIDES AND ATTRACTIONS

waiting as there is lot to see from the vantage point – like the Phantom Manor queue you are up high, so you can watch the activity on the water below. Children may get fidgety as there is no organised entertainment, but the ride is so good they are bound to queue again and again!

Entertainment during queuing:
None.

Visual and audio effects:
Superb.

Worth another ride?
Definitely – but if you ride again immediately, it may not be as thrilling. Come back and do it again at the end of the day – the ride takes on a new dimension at dark.

MARK TWAIN AND MOLLY BROWN STEAMBOATS

Location:
Frontierland

Overall comment:
A good ride on which to take some photographs. Relaxing on a sunny day, but otherwise dull and dreary. One for the grannies.

Ratings:
Adults: ***
Teenagers: *
7–12 year olds: ***

4–7 year olds: ***
Toddlers: ***

Description:
The Molly Brown and Mark Twain paddle steamers take you on a slow, adventureless voyage around Big Thunder Mountain on the Rivers of the Far West. It may not be a thrill a minute, but it is a good opportunity to photograph the hot springs and other sculpted areas and it is very atmospheric and evocative of the era.

Make for the mid-deck (front) bow area and try for a seat – most people bound straight up to the top to find all the seats have gone. If it's raining, there are indoor seated cabins, but this really is a ride to try on a sunny day. It can also be quite romantic at night as a way of relaxing after dinner.

Duration of ride:
12 minutes.

Length of queues:
Up to 20 minutes.
Most people in the sheltered waiting area should board the paddle steamer. If queues are big, don't bother.

Entertainment during queuing:
None, apart from watching the screaming crowds on Thunder Mountain.

Best time of day to go there:
When it is sunny or for relaxation after dinner.

REVIEWS OF RIDES AND ATTRACTIONS

Visual and audio effects:
Most of the commentary and dialogue is in French. The action is "on-shore" – you watch from the ship. Don't stand too near the funnel or you will be blasted by the ship's horn.

Worth another ride?
No.

RIVER ROGUE KEEL BOATS

Location:
Frontierland

Overall comment:
Similar appeal as Mark Twain and Molly Brown Steamboats. Don't bother doing both these rides on the same day.

Ratings:
Adults: ***
Teenagers: *
7–12 year olds: ***
4–7 year olds: ***
Toddlers: ***

Description
Styled like 19th-century keel boats, this is another way to explore the Rivers of the Far West. There are two wooden boats, the *Coyote* and the *Racoon*, both powered by diesel engines and steered by Disney cast members who stand at the back, dressed in long coats, leather boots and big black hats.

Duration of ride:
About eight minutes.

Length of queues:
Up to 45 minutes on a hot day.

Entertainment during queuing:
None.

Best time of day to go there:
When it's sunny. But don't waste time queuing.

Visual and audio effects:
Like the steamboats, all the action is on-shore.

Worth another ride?
No.

INDIAN BIRCHBARK CANOES

Location:
Frontierland

Overall comment:
A more active way to explore the Rivers of the Far West. Relaxing on a warm day. Fun for children.

Ratings:
Adults: ***
Teenagers: ***
7–12 years olds: ****
4–7 year olds: ****
Toddlers: Not suitable

REVIEWS OF RIDES AND ATTRACTIONS

Description:
Paddle around the island in a fibreglass canoe. You sit in pairs with the cast members (one at front and one at back) guiding you. Everyone has a paddle although you get the feeling that the canoe is mainly being propelled along by the paddles of the cast members. On a warm, sunny day it's a relaxing way to view Euro Disney's detailed landscaping both on the shore (watch out for the old-timer relaxing with his barking dog) and the antics of the Railroad. This form of river transport also enables you to take a closer look at the island.

Duration of ride:
About ten minutes.

Length of queues:
Up to 45 minutes. Not worth queuing for more than 20 minutes.

Entertainment during queuing:
None.

Best time of day to go there:
When it's warm.

Visual and audio effects:
Only those animatronics onshore and on the island.

Worth another ride:
No.

PHANTOM MANOR

Location:
Frontierland.

Overall comment:
Don't miss! One of the best and most imaginative of Euro Disney's attractions. Not a high-speed thrill ride but one to be savoured again and again.

Ratings:
Adults: *****
Teenagers: *****
7–12 year olds: *****
4–7 year olds: ***** Not admitted without an adult. Too scary for small or nervous children.
Toddlers: * Too scary.

Description:
Phantom Manor is a large, dejected-looking Victorian house on the top of a hill overlooking the Rivers of the Far West. As you approach its doors, you can hear the wind howling and see how everything in the garden has withered.

A crowd of about 30 are shown into a doorless chamber, a room that eerily elongates itself and where things are obviously not what they seem. You are told that in this room a death has occurred. There is no way out. You must move on to a "doom buggy", a carriage for two which swivels round 180 degrees as you tour the haunted manor.

If you do not like the feeling of creepy crawlies, you will be glad to know that there are no unseen "things" touching you. The scariness is purely

REVIEWS OF RIDES AND ATTRACTIONS

visual and aural. The wedding reception scene is particularly haunting.

If you survive the doom buggy journey, leave the manor and follow the path uphill to the "crypt" to see the Boot Hill Cemetery (look out for the morbidly funny epitaphs) and to oversee the hot springs. This is a good vantage point for photos of the lake – can you spot the coyote on the opposite hill?

Duration of ride:
15–20 minutes.

Length of queues:
Up to 40 minutes. Most of the queuing is under cover.

Entertainment during queuing:
None. But you can watch the Molly Brown Steamboat and the Big Thunder Mountain Railroad. The grounds of the manor are also superbly detailed with gnarled and withered trees, the sound of howling wind, and tiles and cracked paint falling off the eerie house.

Best time of day to go there:
Anytime.

Visual and audio effects:
Disney's finest show of audio-animatronics and visuals, surpassed only by Pirates of the Caribbean.

Worth another ride?
Yes, if only to work out how they do it!

RUSTLER ROUNDUP SHOOTIN' GALLERY

Location:
Frontierland.

Overall comment:
The only attraction inside Euro Disney for which you have to pay. 10F for a rifle – a bit steep for what is just an ordinary side-show.

Ratings:
Adults: *
Teenagers: **
7–12 years olds: **
4–7 years olds: Not allowed.

Description:
A standard fairground electronic shooting gallery – "hit" the bullseye and you activate the exhibit, in this case, a Wild West frontier scene with exploding dynamite and little foxes peeping their heads out of holes.

Like similar electronic games, this is liable to malfunction. Some of the gun coin slots will be taped up. Make sure you put your coin in the right slot and not in that of your neighbour's gun.

For 10F you get an indeterminate number of "bullets". It is difficult to perceive if you or your neighbour have actually hit the target.

Length of queues:
Up to ten minutes.

Entertainment during queuing:
None.

Best time of day to go there:
Anytime, but don't bother queuing.

Visual and audio effects:
Disappointing special effects (you'll get better on Brighton Pier!). The kick of the gun isn't satisfying enough either.

Worth another go?
No. Not worth paying for.

COTTONWOOD CREEK RANCH

Location:
Frontierland.

Overall comment:
Ideal for little children who can stroke their favourite farmyard animals in this spotlessly clean corral.

Ratings:
Adults: *
Teenagers: *
7–12 year olds: ***
4–7 year olds: ****
Toddlers: ****

Description:
Cottonwood Creek Ranch is a small corralled area in which sheep, goats, rabbits, chickens and piglets can be viewed and stroked in a scrupulously clean environment. The rabbit hutch is spacious but has an unattractive grilled floor. The farmyard animals are run-of-the-mill but look healthy and well groomed. Most of the animals are allowed to roam free and will nuzzle your hand for food.

Only see this attraction if you have time to spare or if your youngsters have never touched farmyard animals. Make sure the animals don't chew your camera/handbag!

You are not allowed to feed the animals and strollers must be left outside.

Duration of visit:
As long as you like.

Length of queues:
None.

Entertainment during queuing:
None.

Best time of day to go there:
Anytime. Closes at dusk.

Visual and audio effects:
None, just the real grunts and bleats of the animals!

Worth another visit:
No.

REVIEWS OF RIDES AND ATTRACTIONS

ADVENTURELAND

PIRATES OF THE CARIBBEAN

Location:
Adventureland.

Overall comment:
Don't miss! Even better than the same ride in Florida.

An outstanding indoor boat ride through various audio-animatronic tableaux of pirate scenes.

Good mix of humour and thrills – Disney "imagineering" at its best.

Ratings:
Adults: *****
Teenagers: *****
7–12 year olds: *****
4–7 year olds: ***** for older children in this category. Young ones may be scared.
Toddlers: Not suitable.
Not suitable for pregnant women due to the plunging motion of the boats under attack.

Description:
Enter into the depths of the pirates' underground lair, past tableaux of skeletons and shipwrecked timbers. Board the boat and travel through a succession of pirate scenes.

At the beginning of the journey you glide past the Blue Lagoon restaurant where human diners feast on tropical food. Then it's off to watch the merry audio-animatronic crew chasing maidens, fighting over treasure and swigging from barrels of liquor. Watch out for the eerie eyes (bats/rats) peering at you from dark corners.

This fabulous ride offers roller-coaster thrills too. Your boat hurtles down two slopes, escaping cannonfire. A pirate swings on a rope over your heads.

Don't take children who scare easily, although the ever-present jolly pirates' song lifts the spirits.

Keep your arms inside the boat and expect to be splashed a little.

Duration of ride:
12 minutes.

Length of queues:
Up to one hour. Allow 25 minutes if you join the end of the queue at the entrance. On a hot day, queuing for this ride can be sweaty and claustrophobic.

Entertainment during queuing:
Jolly ho-ho-ho music, eerie sound effects, pirate tableaux.

Best time of day to go there:
Early, as queues will be smaller and you will probably want to go back and do it again.

Visual and audio effects:
Disney's best audio-animatronic ride, rich in atmosphere and packed with thrills.

Worth another ride?
Definitely.

ADVENTURE ISLE

This is divided into two islets joined by a bridge. In the north is Treasure Island, in the south is the Swiss Family Robinson Treehouse. See reviews below.

TREASURE ISLAND

Location:
Adventureland.

Overall comment:
Great fun for young explorers. Older children can play here while parents have coffee in Captain Hook's galley.

Ratings:
Adults: **
Teenagers: **
7–12 year olds: *****
4–7 year olds: *****
Toddlers: ***

Based on:
Treasure Island by Robert Louis Stevenson and *Peter Pan* by J. M. Barrie, both Scottish novelists.

Description:
This island is great fun for children who will enjoy clambering over the precarious bridge and exploring the network of tunnels and underground caves. Walk up to Spyglass Hill which has a series of

vantage points offering a panoramic view of Adventureland (don't forget to take your camera). Young children will enjoy the shuddering suspension bridge overlooking the wrecked galleon. Look through the brass telescopes at each vantage point.

Afterwards, descend into Ben Gunn's Cave to see the stalactites and stalagmites. Or feel your way round Dead Man's Maze, a spooky underground network of tunnels beneath a spectacular waterfall, illuminated by glowing bats' eyes.

Peter Pan fans will enjoy visiting Captain Hook's Pirate Ship. There is a café in the ship or you can take your camera upstairs on deck and let the children play with the ship's wheel and rigging. Near the ship you will see the sinister Skull Rock where you can look across at Captain Hook's Ship through the eye sockets of the "rock".

Duration of visit:
Allow half an hour to explore.

Length of queues:
None.

Entertainment during queuing:
None.

Best time of day to go there:
Anytime.

Visual and audio effects:
A few tableaux and spooky lights in the mazes, but most are "natural".

REVIEWS OF RIDES AND ATTRACTIONS

Worth another visit?
Not unless you have spare time at the end of your visit.

SWISS FAMILY ROBINSON TREEHOUSE

Location:
Adventureland.

Overall comment:
Tree-top home built by the shipwrecked Robinson family. A fine example of Disney imagineering.

Ratings:
Adults: ****
Teenagers: ****
7–12 year olds: *****
4–7 year olds: ****
Toddlers: * (too many steps to contend with)
Not suitable for people who have problems walking or climbing stairs.

Based on:
Swiss Family Robinson by Johann David Wyss.

Description:
This 90-foot tree, in the heart of Adventureland, is a miracle of Disney imagineering as it is entirely man-made, from its roots to its leaves. Based on the 1960s real-life Disney adventure film, this depicts the house built by the Robinsons when they were shipwrecked on their desert island. The rooms are packed with detail such as the old books and maps

in the library, and the water wheel and water supply fashioned from bamboo.

It really captures the imagination of what living in a treehouse could be like and makes you realise how lucky the Robinsons were to have salvaged so much undamaged furniture from their ship. The climate must have been a far cry from Parisian temperatures for the Robinsons to have endured an open-air bedroom!

Afterwards it's also fun to explore The Root Cellar (Le Ventre de la Terre), a dark maze under the roots of the tree. Lit by flickering lamps, it's difficult to see where you are walking and you are likely to bump into people. In the centre, you can look up at the Treehouse. Not for the claustrophobic or those who are afraid of the dark!

Duration of visit:
Allow 20 minutes to walk slowly round.

Length of queues:
You may have to wait for up to 15 minutes at the entrance if people congest inside.

Entertainment during queuing:
None.

Best time of day to go there:
Anytime, preferably not right at the end of the day when you feel too weary to walk to the top!

Visual and audio effects:
None, apart from the visible "engineering".

Worth another visit?
Not really.

FANTASYLAND

SLEEPING BEAUTY'S CASTLE

Location:
Fantasyland.

Overall comment:
Don't miss. Stunningly designed castle and central landmark of Euro Disney.

Ratings:
Adults: *****
Teenagers: *****
7–12 year olds: *****
4–7 year olds: *****
Toddlers: *** (avoid the cellar, as young children may be frightened by the dragon)

Based on:
Sleeping Beauty by Frenchman Charles Perrault.

Description:
This beautiful ornate and magical castle is the central landmark of Fantasyland and Euro Disney and a worthwhile attraction in itself. It is based on a European castle, complete with tapestries, vaulted ceilings, a moat, a waterfall and a cellar where a dragon lurks.

Children will never be content with a tour of your average European castle after this! Beautifully designed inside and out, the stained-glass windows depict the story of Sleeping Beauty.

After viewing the tapestries and stained-glass windows on the first floor, don't forget to go downstairs to the dragon's lair (la tanière du dragon) where the smoke-breathing, red-eyed dragon raises its head from a pool, a broken chain dangling from its neck, its long tail flicking menacingly.

Length of queues:
None.

Entertainment during queuing:
Not applicable.

Best time of day to go there:
As you don't have to queue for this attraction, don't waste time touring the castle when you first arrive at the park. Come back to walk round at leisure when the other rides are busier.

Visual and audio effects:
The animatronic dragon is a treat. A deep-throated roar and acrid smoke adds to the chilling effect. The castle has also been specially designed with forced perspective so that the tallest tower (45m) looks much taller than it actually is.

Worth another visit?
Yes, it's even more atmospheric and beautiful at dark.

SNOW WHITE AND THE SEVEN DWARFS

Location:
Fantasyland.

Overall comment:
More interesting than next door's Pinocchio Adventures, but too scary for very little children. These two rides are very similar, so choose one or the other depending on your child's age and sensitivity and the length of the queues.

Ratings:
Adults: ***
Teenagers: *
7–12 year olds: *****
4–7 years olds: ***** (smaller, sensitive children may be scared)
Toddlers: * (too scary)

Based on:
The German fairytale by the Grimm brothers.

Description:
A fast-moving indoor ride in seated trolleys named after the Seven Dwarfs. This is a great ride for children, with enough detail to keep adults amused. You pass through a series of rooms depicting scenes from the Snow White film. Parents be warned: the ride concentrates on the wicked witch and some scenes, particularly the one in the forest where it looks as though you are going to be entangled by the evil trees, are frightening! The ride moves a little too quickly for adults who will be disappointed not to have more time to take in

all the intricate detail. You may want to ride again while junior wants to run off next door to see Pinocchio!

Duration of ride:
Three minutes.

Length of queues:
Up to 45 minutes.

Entertainment during queuing:
None.

Best time of day to go there:
Early, while others are still lingering in Sleeping Beauty's Castle, or during the Parade.

Visual and audio effects:
Great creepy sound effects, and jolly tunes from the film. After the colour imagery of the opening tableaux (and in keeping with the Pinocchio ride) most of the scenes are dark and gloomy, like a mystical "Ghost Train" ride.

Worth another ride?
Yes, it's all over too quickly.

PINOCCHIO'S ADVENTURES

Location:
Fantasyland.

Overall comment:
Similar to Snow White and the Seven Dwarfs (*see page 103*) but less scary and so more suitable for

REVIEWS OF RIDES AND ATTRACTIONS

little children. Choose one or the other depending on your child's age and sensitivity and the length of the queues.

Ratings:
Adults: **
Teenagers: *
7–12 year olds: ****
4–7 year olds: *****
Toddlers: Very small children may be scared.

Based on:
Italian fairytale by Carlo Collodi.

Description:
Great ride for the under-sevens especially if they've seen the film and know the story and characters. Not as scary as Snow White, but again the ride concentrates on the more frightening scenes from the film such as the fairground, the puppetteer's cages and the whale. Very young children may not like it!

Duration of ride:
Three minutes.

Length of queues:
Fast-moving. Allow 15–20 minutes if busy.

Entertainment during queuing:
None.

Best time of day to go there:
Early, while people are still lingering in Main Street USA or Sleeping Beauty's Castle, or during the Parade.

Visual and audio effects:
Starts with jolly tunes, giving way to scary sound effects once in the fairground scene. The best effect is of the whale raising its head to swallow you (despite a warning from Jiminy Cricket).

Worth another ride?
Yes, if it's your child's favourite story.

PETER PAN'S FLIGHT

Location:
Fantasyland.

Overall comment:
Don't miss! At last, you too have a chance to fly like Peter Pan over the rooftops of London. A visually thrilling ride that adults will enjoy as much as children.

Ratings:
Adults: *****
Teenagers: ****
7–12 year olds: *****
4–7 year olds: ***** Must be accompanied by an adult.
Toddlers: *** (may be scared)

Based on:
Peter Pan by J. M. Barrie.

Description:
Magical. Disney at its best. This is one of the most popular rides at Euro Disney, and once children

have tried it they usually want to do it again and again. The reason for its success is that it really does make you feel as though you are flying in a pirate ship above the rooftops and twinkling lights of London. The ship is suspended from above and whisks you through a series of tableaux from the Peter Pan film – the children's bedroom, out of the window, through the clouds to Never-Never-Land.

Duration of ride:
Four minutes.

Length of queues:
Up to one and a half hours at peak times. This is one of the worst rides in Euro Disney for queuing.

Entertainment during queuing:
None.

Best time of day to go there:
If you are with children, as soon as you get to the park, otherwise during the Parade. A good time for adults is late at night, just before the park closes.

Visual and audio effects:
Visually one of Disney's best rides in Fantasyland.

Worth another ride:
Yes, definitely.

LANCELOT'S CAROUSEL

Location:
Fantasyland.

Overall comment:
A beautifully ornate merry-go-round, delightful for children on a sunny day but miserable when it is wet and windy.

Ratings:
Adults: **
Teenagers: *
7–12 year olds: **
4–7 year olds: ****
Toddlers: *****

Description:
This colourful carousel adds to the fairground atmosphere of Fantasyland. The horses are beautifully ornate with gilt manes, their flanks embossed with brightly coloured gems and their hooves with shoes of silver, bronze or shiny gold. Allegedly Elizabeth Taylor's favourite ride.

The horses on the outside are the grandest. Toddlers seem to love this ride. There are leather straps to hold the children tight.

Children who are at the end of the queue may be disappointed to end up in one of the carriages – large semi-circular seated areas between the horses. As there is so much of novelty value elsewhere, don't waste time queuing for what is basically a traditional fairground ride.

REVIEWS OF RIDES AND ATTRACTIONS

Duration of ride:
90 seconds.

Length of queues:
Up to 15 minutes on a sunny day.

Entertainment during queuing:
None.

Best time of day to go there:
Anytime. After dark is particularly romantic.

Visual and audio effects:
Disney songs set to carousel arrangements.

Worth another ride?
No.

DUMBO THE FLYING ELEPHANT

Location:
Fantasyland.

Overall comment:
Traditional high-flying fairground ride with a Dumbo theme. Great fun for little ones.

Ratings:
Adults: **
Teenagers: *
7–12 year olds: ***
4–7 year olds ***** Must be accompanied by an adult.

Toddlers: *** Must be accompanied by an adult.
Under-ones not allowed.
Some toddlers may be scared.

Description:
Take to the skies with big-eared Dumbo, under the supervision of Timothy Mouse who conducts the flight standing at the top of a hot-air balloon. Each flying baby elephant seats two or three passengers. You can control how high your Dumbo flies up and down.

Similar ride to Orbitron, aimed at small children and without the visual impact of Orbitron's design.

Duration of ride:
Two minutes.

Length of queues:
Up to 45 minutes.

Entertainment during queuing:
None.

Best time of day to go there:
Anytime.

Visual and audio effects:
None.

Worth another ride?
Yes, for children. Also fun at night.

REVIEWS OF RIDES AND ATTRACTIONS

MAD HATTER'S TEACUPS

Location:
Fantasyland.

Overall comment:
Traditional fairground ride, with giant cups that whirl you round.

Ratings:
Adults: ***
Teenagers: ****
7–12 year olds: *****
4–7 year olds: *****
Toddlers: ** (too fast)
Not suitable for pregnant women.

Based on:
Alice in Wonderland by Lewis Carroll.

Description:
Eighteen giant teacups (each of which can hold a family of five) whirl round in circles under a covered pagoda decorated with Chinese lanterns. The teacup spins one way while the saucer turns in the opposite direction. You have some control over the spinning speed but this is not one to do after a big meal or ice-cream!

This ride offers more thrills than Dumbo or Autopia and is more popular with children up to mid-teens.

One to head for if it's wet – even the queuing is under cover.

Duration of ride:
90 seconds.

Length of queues:
Less than most other rides in Fantasyland. Up to 20–30 minutes.

Entertainment during queuing:
None.

Best time of day to go there:
Anytime, but preferably not after eating!

Visual and audio effects:
Fairground music.

Worth another ride?
No.

ALICE'S CURIOUS LABYRINTH

Location:
Fantasyland.

Overall comment:
An outdoor, walkthrough attraction for all the family and an ideal spot to take photos. Low on thrills, more one to do at leisure.

Ratings:
Adults: ****
Teenagers: **
7–12 year olds: ****
4–7 year olds: ****

REVIEWS OF RIDES AND ATTRACTIONS

Toddlers: ****

Based on:
Alice in Wonderland by Lewis Carroll.

Description:
This outdoor attraction is easily ignored by those queuing for the carriage rides at the entrance to Fantasyland, but it is great fun for the under-12s. It is not a complex maze in the style of Hampton Court, but more a corridor between real hedges and through plastic ivy arches, leading to the Queen of Hearts' castle at the centre.

Children will love the squeaks and whistles emanating from the hedges and the Alice characters peering at them from corners.

The vantage points from the castle also offer what must be the prettiest picture opportunities of all in Euro Disney so do not forget your camera. Don't worry if you hate the frustration of wrong turnings in mazes – it's impossible to get lost in this one and it offers a pleasant stroll through mostly real greenery.

Duration of visit:
Allow 20 minutes.

Length of queues:
Up to 20 minutes at peak times.

Entertainment during queuing:
None.

Best time of day to go there:
Anytime, but preferably when it is sunny.

Visual and audio effects:
A few "noises" from hidden speakers in the hedges. Disappointingly few of the characters move.

Worth another visit?
No.

IT'S A SMALL WORLD

Location:
Fantasyland

Overall comment:
A leisurely boat ride through a world of beautifully costumed singing and dancing dolls. A good one for small children and aunties.

Ratings:
Adults: ****
Teenagers: **
7–12 year olds: ****
4–7 year olds: *****
Toddlers: *****

Description:
"It's A Small World" was designed by Walt Disney to be "the happiest cruise that ever sailed round the world". Your cruise starts at London Bridge and travels through the five continents. This is the sort of ride that you either love or hate. Thrill-seekers will find it deadly dull. Others, however,

will be enchanted by the musical dolls who are lavishly costumed in the style of their country. The song they sing is one of those infuriating ones that can never be forgotten! Young children will find it educational to identify which countries the dolls are representing. It is also a cosy ride to do on a cold day.

After disembarking from your indoor world cruise, you can spend another couple of minutes walking through a village of model houses. The idea is that you peer through the windows and watch the different uses of the telephone in modern society. Although this is a blatant plug for telecommunications, it is fun for very little children as the windows are arranged at different heights so that they have to squat down to look through the ones near the floor and ask mummy and daddy to lift them up high so they can see through the ones in the tall buildings.

Duration of ride:
Seven minutes. Allow another five to ten minutes to look round the houses.

Length of queues:
Fast-moving. Allow 30 minutes at peak time.

Entertainment during queuing:
None.

Best time of day to go there:
Anytime, but if it looks busy, go back during the Parade.

Visual and audio effects:
Nothing very sophisticated, just dancing dolls in wonderfully detailed national costumes.

Worth another ride?
Yes.

DISCOVERYLAND

STAR TOURS

Location:
Discoveryland.

Overall comment:
Don't miss! Superbly thrilling.

Star ratings:
Adults: *****
Teenagers: *****
7–12 year olds: *****
4–7 year olds: ** Should be accompanied by an adult. Small children may be scared.
Toddlers: Children under three not allowed.
Not suitable for pregnant women or anyone who suffers from back, neck or muscular problems.

Based on:
George Lucas *Star Wars* movies.

Description:
This ride owes much to the imagination of Disney and of the film-maker George Lucas, employing Lucas' characters and sets as well as the thrilling music and effects of his *Star Wars* movies. Disney

have used these to create all the thrills and spills of being a passenger in one of the spaceships, using a specially made film of a journey into space in which you take part.

Before boarding your ship (each of the six ships has a capacity of 40 people) you are briefed for three minutes about safety instructions. The dialogue for this is in French with English subtitles. The doors slide open and you enter your ship, take your seat and fasten your belt.

A robot welcomes you as your pilot and the screen shield lifts to reveal a film screen. The android speaks French, although there are also brief interruptions from the Control Centre in English.

You soon find out that this is your robot pilot's first flight! Be prepared for a lot of thrills and spills as you are rocketed into space with your inexperienced pilot trying to manoeuvre you past meteorites and all sorts of adventures including an inter-galactic battle.

Not a ride for the claustrophobic – I nearly had to pull the emergency handle! Also, not advisable for anyone suffering from motion sickness.

Duration of ride:
Six minutes.

Length of queues:
Up to an hour and a half at peak times. Expect 15 minutes from the first robot tableau.

Entertainment during queuing:
Queuing takes place indoors through corridors of an orbital space station where you watch moving robots repairing spaceships. Dialogue is in French

and English. The queue is slow-moving but there is lots of atmosphere with airport-type announcements over the tannoy and spacecraft debris to look at in a futuristic space repair shop setting.

As in the movies, the robots are cute and witty.

Best time of day to go there:
First thing.

Visual and audio effects:
The visual effects are superb both while queuing and during the ride. The film effects are first rate, as befits the stature of the *Star Wars* movies.

Worth another ride?
Yes. Several! Although you must expect the overall sensation to be diminished with repeated rides. The first ride is always the best!

LE VISIONARIUM

Location:
Discoveryland.

Overall comment:
Don't miss! Superb 360-degree surround-vision film, more scenic than thrilling.

Ratings:
Adults: *****
Teenagers: ****
7–12 year olds: ****
4–7 year olds: ***
Toddlers: Not suitable.

REVIEWS OF RIDES AND ATTRACTIONS

Description:
This is one of the best attractions which has been especially devised for Euro Disney, not just imported from the States. This 360-degree film is packed with European influences and references to its great inventors, as well as some great footage of European towns and countryside.

Have a rest and a snack before queuing for Le Visionarium as you will be on your feet for half-an-hour inside.

Queuing is half under cover before you are shown through the doors into a waiting area – not empty like Captain EO, but facing a wall of video screens. This is La Banque de l'Image. Flying machines, ships, undersea vessels, spacecraft and astronauts hang from the ceiling while a wall display shows inventions of the last century. The room is a celebration principally of the works of H. G. Wells and Jules Verne. A countdown digital clock shows the time lapsing until show time (eight minutes before the auditorium doors open). Meanwhile the wallscreen shows images of transport from years gone by.

Your host is The Timekeeper who introduces you to his robotic friend 9-Eye. You are shown into a large circular room with nine film screens used to portray the film footage as seen through 9-Eye.

There are no seats and you stand in rows with your own headset should you need to listen to the dialogue in English, German or Italian.

The Timekeeper then takes you and Jules Verne (played by actor Michel Piccoli) on a journey back through time starting with the Dinosaur Age and moving into the future. The impact of the film is outstanding and you really feel as though you are travelling through time even though you are standing still. The glimpse of Paris in 100 years' time is overwhelming and the detail in the film demands you see it a second time. One niggle is a hillside battle which we are told is between the Scots and the Brits! The film stars Jeremy Irons and Gerard Depardieu.

Duration of visit:
30 minutes.

Length of queues:
Up to 20 minutes.

Entertainment during queuing:
None outside but film in waiting area.

Best time of day to go there:
Anytime.

Visual and audio effects:
Excellent film effects along the lines of Circlevision at Epcot in Florida. More scenic than thrilling.

Worth another visit?
Definitely, as there is so much detail to absorb.

CINEMAGIQUE: CAPTAIN EO

Location:
Discoveryland.

REVIEWS OF RIDES AND ATTRACTIONS

Overall comment:
Raucous 3-D film which will delight fans of Michael Jackson, *Star Wars*, or both.

Ratings:
Adults: ***
Teenagers: *****
7–12 year olds: *****
4–7 year olds: *** (May be scared by a villainess who resembles a cross between a giant spider and Freddy Krueger.)
Toddlers: not suitable.
Not suitable for people with sensitive hearing.

Description:
A 20-minute 3-D film and pastiche of *Star Wars* featuring a crew of cuddly animals, a curiously-gruff robot styled as a one-legged metallic Admiral, Michael Jackson as Captain EO and Anjelica Huston as the Supreme Leader.

The storyline takes EO and his crew into battle with an enemy craft before crash landing on a foreign planet and coming face to face with an array of villains.

The 3-D effects are augmented by flashing lights set in the ceiling of the auditorium, surround-sound and a searchlight which at one point sweeps the audience. Adults will find it too loud and young children may be frightened. The 3-D glasses handed out at the entrance can be fitted over your own specs. Connoisseurs of pop videos will feel they've seen it all before but perhaps not at this volume, or, of course, in 3-D.

Disappointing for the French that no effort has

been made to dub the dialogue into their own language – although the story is almost irrelevant.

Reviewer's tip: When filing into the auditorium, people will inevitably sit down in the middle, despite being told to move right along (viewing of the film is the same from all seats). Best way to deal with these people is to tread on their feet as you squeeze past.

Duration of film:
About 20 minutes.

Length of queues:
Up to one hour at peak times.

Entertainment during queuing:
None, and it's mostly outdoors and miserable in the wet. Take a brolly and a poncho.

Best time of day to go there:
Anytime.

Visual and audio effects:
Great 3-D, although to my eyes it was never in sharp focus. It all adds up to an extended pop video for Jackson. Main song is one specially written for this film, a rather repetitive pop chant but he closes with his popular *Another Part of Me*. It's all very loud and the dialogue (all English) is not always easy to make out.

Worth another viewing?
No.

ORBITRON

Location:
Discoveryland.

Overall comment:
An average fairground ride, low on thrills but beautifully designed.

Ratings:
Adults: **
Teenagers: **
7–12 year olds: ***
4–7 year olds: ****
Toddlers: **

Description:
Fairground-goers will no doubt have come across this type of flying machine-spaceship ride before.

Twelve ships, each with a capacity for three (at a squeeze), travel round a globe. Press the control lever forward to go up, pull it towards you to descend.

As it only lasts a couple of minutes, you won't be bored, but it has little to offer the thrill-seekers. Children will enjoy pulling the lever back and forwards to create an up and down ride as you whizz past the beautifully ornate metallic "moons" of Orbitron.

Duration of ride:
Two minutes.

Length of queues:
Up to 45 minutes at peak times. The ride can only take, on average, 24 people per two minutes.

Entertainment during queuing:
None.

Best time of day to go there:
Anytime.

Visual and audio effects:
More a visual spectacle for onlookers. Once aboard, there isn't much sensation at all and the outlook on to the park is nothing special.

Worth another ride?
No.

AUTOPIA

Location:
Discoveryland.

Overall comment:
Boring for adults but a chance for children to take the wheel of a futuristic car, and drive it round a curving rail-track.

Ratings:
Adults: *
Teenagers: ***
7–12 year olds: ****
4–7 year olds: *** There is a height restriction for this ride.

Toddlers: Not suitable for very little children. Under-ones not allowed.
Not suitable for pregnant women, people with back, neck or muscular problems.

Description:
The main appeal of this ride is that it enables children and teenagers to drive an open-topped racing-style two-seater car in total safety around a curving rail-track. Adults who have a driving licence will find it frustratingly slow and rather dull! The only control is the drive-pedal which can't be called an accelerator as there is only one speed – "slow"! You don't really need to steer, as there's a metal rail under the car guiding you. It's not even as much fun as dodgems, because you are not allowed to nudge the car in front.

Duration of ride:
Two minutes.

Length of queues:
Up to 30–45 minutes. Allow 15 minutes from the circular seated area.

Entertainment during queuing:
None, apart from watching the cars go round.

Best time of day to go there:
Anytime.

Visual and audio effects:
A satisfying engine roar when you press the pedal, but little to see apart from some futuristic billboards lining the track.

Worth another ride?
No.

CHAPTER SEVEN

THE UNOFFICIAL RESTAURANT GUIDE

Eating out is always an important part of any holiday and at Euro Disney if you don't know where to go this can work out a very costly and frustrating experience!

In this chapter we give you plenty of tips on eating out, review all the restaurants in the park and suggest the best value and most interesting places for you to go. We have also reviewed the restaurants in Festival Disney and highlighted the best places to eat in the hotels. Please note that all prices and menus are subject to change.

RESTAURANT TIPS

We found that the most economical approach to eating in the park was to grab a snack from a speciality cart or fast-food restaurant at lunchtime and then relax in one of the more expensive table-service restaurants at night. Eating in the park at night also enables you to make the most of your entrance pass as, if you eat early (6.30–7pm), you can then do your favourite rides again at night.

The restaurants in the park are considerably cheaper than those in Festival Disney, but the park restaurants are not licensed to serve alcohol. If you want to avoid totting up a big bill with your evening meal in the park, say no to the house "mocktails" (non-alcoholic cocktails) as these are about 30F each.

All the restaurants in Euro Disney have special menus for children, at substantially cheaper rates, offering smaller portions and simpler food.

The fast-food restaurants in Euro Disney are quite unique in their decor. Many of them look like proper table-service restaurants from the outside. Feel free to sit at any of the tables on the restaurant terraces, whether you are eating there or not. Unlike Paris, there is no charge at Disney to just sit down, soak up the sun and watch the world go by.

The portions in the fast-food restaurants are usually small, encouraging you to "graze" throughout the day. Try to stagger your eating times so that you avoid the lunchtime crush (12.30–2pm). If you want to eat at a table-service restaurant, make your reservation in person after 11am. Most of the restaurants in the park are open from 11am (some open even earlier) until the park closes.

Have your coffee breaks in fast-food restaurants and snack bars (5F for a coffee). You will pay twice this in the plusher establishments such as Plaza Gardens.

Finally, you are not allowed to bring food and drink into the park. Be warned: they search your bags! Picnic areas are located outside the park near the car park, although it is doubtful that you will want to leave the park in the day. If you do, make sure you get your hand stamped for re-entry.

TOP RESTAURANTS

Below is our personal selection of the best places to eat at Euro Disney.

BEST FOR BREAKFAST

Character Breakfasts (Hotel Disneyland, Hotel New York and Newport Bay Club)
The top Disney hotels all do "character breakfasts" for 140F (105F for the under-tens). These are buffet breakfasts with special appearances from Disney characters. Expect to see two or three characters during an hour's breakfast. It is good value if you are very hungry, as you can help yourself to as much as you want from the lavish buffet (dishes include scrambled eggs, smoked salmon, sausages, hash browns, bacon, cereals, yoghurts and a wide selection of fruits). Young children particularly enjoy this type of breakfast as they get a chance to see their favourite characters before the day has even begun.

Parkside Diner (Hotel New York)
This American-style diner offers a varied breakfast menu. For example, their Fitness Breakfast (110F) comprises a platter of fresh fruit, toasted honey granola, low fat yoghurt, coffee or tea, fresh fruit juice. Lady Liberty Breakfast (115F) offers eggs, sausages, hash browns, bakery basket, coffee or tea and fresh fruit juice. 7th Avenue Special (120F) comprises lox, bagel and cream cheese with coffee or tea with fruit juice.

Chuckwagon Café (Hotel Cheyenne)
Good place for a reasonably priced substantial breakfast. Like all the meals here, breakfast is self-service from various food carts. Breakfast dishes include steaming hot porridge, large bowls of fresh fruit and berries, pancakes with maple syrup.

Cable Car Bake Shop (Main Street USA)
If you want to have a quick breakfast in the park, you can grab a coffee and croissant or muffin at this Main Street bakery.

Plaza Gardens (Main Street USA)
This Victorian-style buffet restaurant is the place to come to if you want a substantial breakfast in the park. Dishes include fresh fruit platters and lox and cream cheese bagels.

BEST FOR LUNCH

Speciality carts
The cheapest food in Euro Disney is from speciality carts in the park. Expect to pay 15F for a jacket

potato with chilli con carne or melted cheese at **Railroad Spike** (FRONTIERLAND), 15F for a beef or chicken brochette from the stall by the Blue **Lagoon Restaurant** (ADVENTURELAND), 18F for a cheese and ham sandwich at a stall near the **Bazaar** (ADVENTURELAND), 20F for a hot-dog from a stall in DISCOVERYLAND.

Victoria's Homestyle Cooking (Main Street USA)
One of the prettiest and quietest counter-service restaurants. Pot pies, hot from the oven from 26F.

Walt's Terrace (Main Street USA)
Special terrace menu at this top-class restaurant. Very pleasant on a hot day. Main courses included crabcakes (95F), seafood gratin (90F) and roast guinea fowl (80F). Desserts include key lime pie (30F) and cheesecake (40F).

Plaza Gardens (Main Street USA)
Self-service restaurant with high quality food and beautiful furnishings. Choice of salads, cold dishes such as poached salmon and freshly prepared hot dishes.

Casey's Corner (Main Street USA)
The place to come for hot-dogs and chocolate brownies. Seating inside and out. Popular with teenagers.

Pizzeria Bella Notte (Fantasyland)
Fast food pasta and pizza restaurant. Small but tasty portions.

Carnegie's (Festival Disney)
Cheapest place for lunch if you are shopping in Festival Disney. Eat in or take away. New York-style sandwiches and bagels.

BEST FOR DINNER

Lucky Nugget Saloon (Frontierland)
Good food and entertainment. Fun for all the family.

Explorer's Club (Adventureland)
Wonderfully imaginative jungle setting. Exotic food.

Blue Lagoon (Adventureland)
Moonlit Caribbean-style restaurant for romantic twosomes.

Walt's (Main Street USA)
Stylish American themed restaurant with excellent food and first class service.

Carnegie's (Festival Disney)
New York-style deli good for a take-away or sit-down lunch if you are shopping in Festival Disney.

Key West (Festival Disney)
Large seafood restaurant overlooking Lake Buena Vista, specialising in crab dishes.

Club Manhattan (Hotel New York)
Elegant restaurant for that special dîner-à-deux. Styled on the Rainbow Room in New York.

THE UNOFFICIAL RESTAURANT GUIDE

Chuck Wagon Café (Hotel Cheyenne)
Good place for reasonably priced family supper in fun Wild West atmosphere. Huge plate of barbecued food (89F).

Crockett's Tavern (Camp Davy Crockett)
Small pine-decked restaurant serving excellent burgers, with a fresh salad bar, and other simple fare for family dinners.

A GUIDE TO THE RESTAURANTS IN THE THEME PARK

All the table-service and fast-food restaurants have been awarded a star rating (* to *****). This is based on the atmosphere, service and quality of food.

We have also given an approximate indication of what you would expect to pay for two adults for dîner-à-deux in the table-service restaurants. This is based on a three-course meal with soft drinks. In the fast-food restaurants, we have just highlighted prices of individual dishes as you probably won't want a three-course lunch.

MAIN STREET USA

Table-Service Restaurants:

WALT'S
Star rating: *****
Dîner-à-deux: 350F–450F.
According to our waiter this is the "top" restaurant in Euro Disney and the food and service was certainly of a high standard. It is an elegant res-

133

taurant, divided into several small, intimate, themed dining-rooms. We sat upstairs in Frontierland, an old-fashioned Wild West-style reading room with Red Indians on the wall and leatherbound Wild West books on the shelves. The intimate atmosphere is enhanced by candlelight, taped violin music and swagged velvet curtains.

Our starter was a tangy salad comprising shrimps, cherry tomatoes, Texan nuts and lettuce, tossed in a herb dressing and prepared freshly in front of us. Go easy on the speciality breads as there is plenty of food still to come and you want to leave room for one of their rich desserts! For a main course we tried the almond chicken with broccoli and fetuccini (tasty but very rich) and scampi with pasta (not so pleasing – tepid and the sauce tasted like ketchup).

Children may find the atmosphere rather formal, but the staff are exceptionally friendly and good with babies.

The restaurant also has a terrace outside offering a smaller selection of dishes and good for an alfresco lunch.

Self-Service Restaurants:

PLAZA GARDENS
Star rating: *****
Diner-à-deux: 200F–275F
This is a very elegant Victorian-style restaurant with buffet service. Velvet-backed chairs, cream and gilt pillars, cloth serviettes and silver cutlery make this the smartest self-service restaurant in Euro Disney. The food is excellent whether you want a healthy breakfast, a light lunch or a three-

course dinner. Prices, however, are high, and you pay twice as much for a coffee here as you do at any of the fast-food restaurants. It also gets very busy at lunchtime so try to come early (11.30am) or after the midday crowds (2pm).

Main dishes on the menu include Caesar salad, poached salmon platter, grilled chicken breast, roast veal, Maryland Crabcakes, sirloin steak, followed by a big selection of desserts such as chocolate mousse or fresh fruit shortcake.

There is a terrace for eating outside in the summer.

Fast-Food Restaurants:

MARKET HOUSE DELI
Star rating: ***
Old-fashioned deli which specialises in giant, freshly made sandwiches (30F) with hot pastrami, turkey or roast beef. As it is centrally located on Main Street, queues for this restaurant are often very long.

VICTORIA'S HOME-STYLE COOKING
Star rating: *****
This is one of the most attractive fast-food restaurants in Euro Disney and as it is slightly tucked out of sight at the top of the Discovery Arcade, it doesn't become so busy as some of the other Main Street restaurants.

It's decorated like a pretty Victorian boarding house and specialises in pot pies, hot from the oven. Choose between beef and vegetable (38F), chicken and vegetable (32F), seafood and vegetable (35F) or just plain vegetable pie (26F).

You can eat inside or out.

CASEY'S CORNER
Star rating: *****
Teenagers will particularly enjoy this atmospheric hot-dog haunt with its baseball-themed decor. Sit inside or out. The hot-dogs here are so good it is even busy at breakfast! Their chocolate brownies are also delicious. The menu includes hot-dogs (20F), chilli-dogs (26F), foot-long cheese-dogs (30F) and chicken-dogs (20F), chips (5F), coleslaw (7,50F), brownies (12F).

Snacks:

THE ICE-CREAM COMPANY
Small ice-cream kiosk in Discovery Arcade. One scoop 10F, two scoops 16F in cones or dishes.

THE COFFEE GRINDER
Small coffee bar in Discovery Arcade. Coffee (5F), iced coffee (6F).

COOKIE KITCHEN
Small stall with service both from the Main Street counter and inside the Cable Car Bake Shop. Freshly baked muffins, brownies, cookies and coffee.

CABLE CAR BAKE SHOP
Old-fashioned San Francisco-style bake shop with a few tables inside. Freshly baked croissants and cakes. Coffee.

THE GIBSON GIRL ICE-CREAM PARLOUR
Old-fashioned ice-cream parlour at the top of Main Street with tables both inside and out. A limited menu comprises banana split (38F), hot fudge

sundae (30F), sundae framboise (28F), milkshake (27F) and ice-cream float (22F).

FRONTIERLAND

Table-Service Restaurants:

THE LUCKY NUGGET SALOON
Overall Star rating: ****
Dîner-à-deux: 400F

At 200F per head, this restaurant is good value if you want to see a show with your meal. The room is beautifully designed like a revue hall with tables on the floor at the front for groups of three or more, and counter seats behind for couples or people on their own.

They don't give you much of a starter – just a bowl of tortilla chips with chilli and guacamole dips. You then have a choice of prime rib of beef (excellent) or barbecued chicken and spare ribs. Both come served with jacket potatoes and vegetables. Dessert is good old-fashioned apple pie with ice-cream.

The 30-minute revue show (*see page 176 for review*) starts about an hour after the doors open.

SILVER SPUR STEAKHOUSE
Overall Star Rating: ***
Dîner-à-deux: 400F–500F

This is not a very interesting table-service restaurant, a plain old-fashioned steakhouse with nothing apart from the card-playing magician to keep the kids amused. The decor is plush with an open grill, chandeliers and rather a formal, stuffy atmosphere.

For starters there are buffalo wings baked in garlic. You then have a choice of good quality steaks, all of which are Angus meats from Aberdeen. Desserts include cheesecake and pecan pie.

Not very exciting, but perfectly adequate if you just want a good slice of steak.

Fast-Food Restaurants:

FUENTE DEL ORO
Star rating: ****
Attractively designed Mexican cantina with tables inside and out and entertainment from the Fuente del Oro Mariachis band (the only Disney cast members allowed to have moustaches!).

Menu includes fajitas (46F), tacos (37F), chilli con carne (32F), taco salad (28F). Also tortilla chips with guacamole (5F).

COWBOY COOKOUT BARBECUE
Star rating: *****
Huge barn-style restaurant, cosy on a cold day, with wagon wheels on the walls, wooden tables and chairs, and a small stage where the Cowhand Band performs. Fun for kids. Menu includes chicken and chips (41F), pork ribs and chips (44F), cheeseburger and chips (35F), chilli with corn bread (32F) and smoked chicken salad (32F). Apple pie (12F) or ice-cream sandwich (15F) for dessert.

LAST CHANCE CAFÉ
Star rating: **
Located between Silver Spur Steakhouse and Lucky Nugget Saloon.

Tables inside or outside overlooking Thunder

Mountain. Hot beef sandwiches and chips (32F), smoked BBQ turkey leg (36F), black bean soup (10F), followed by apple pie (12F) or ice-cream sandwich (15F).

ADVENTURELAND

Table-Service Restaurants:

EXPLORER'S CLUB
Overall star rating: *****
Dîner-à-deux: 300F–400F

This is a fun, atmospheric place to eat, with good size portions and an interesting menu.

It's relaxing from the moment you walk up the junglefied path. You wait for a table in a rocking chair inside a green and white summer house building. Waiters are dressed in safari kit, there is tropical music playing in the background and a giant tree in the middle of the restaurant. In summer, you can eat outside on the verandah amongst tropical trees.

The menu starts with a plate of salamis and smoked ham with exotic fruits such as papaya and figs. This is accompanied by a plate of Italian onion bread with spicy tomato sauce. For a main course, choose between dishes such as baked fish in banana leaf, grilled swordfish, grilled young chicken in coconut sauce or braised rabbit with peppers. If you still have room, you can finish off with a river-raft sundae, jungle camp cake or poached pear with coconut ice-cream.

Safari meals for children include Bombay Burger and french fries, ham and pasta or fish fries.

In the evening look out for Dr Livingstone, a strolling entertainer.

BLUE LAGOON RESTAURANT
Overall star rating: *****
Dîner-à-deux: 350–450F

You will probably be tempted to eat at this romantic underground restaurant when you pass by on the Pirates of the Caribbean ride. It should be a cool, relaxing place to come on a hot summer's evening. We went when it was pouring with rain outside and it seemed damp and cold.

It has been imaginatively designed, Caribbean-style, complete with white sand beach, bamboo furnishings and a terrace overlooking the water where the pirate boats glide by. A steel band plays in the evening.

The restaurant specialises in seafood. The starter comprises a selection of smoked fishes. Then choose between dishes such as grilled tiger prawns, swordfish, red snapper or chicken and shrimp curry. For dessert, there are Jamaican chippies with coconut ice-cream, rum cake in pineapple sauce or swashbuckler's sundae.

A place for dinner rather than lunch. Although it is the most romantic of the Disney restaurants, ideal for dîner-à-deux, children will enjoy the chance to watch the boats passing.

Fast-Food Restaurants:

AUX EPICES ENCHANTÉES
Star rating: *****
From the outside this looks like a proper restaurant with its beautiful exotic design. It is actu-

ally a fast-food restaurant (tables inside and out) with an interesting menu comprising dishes such as lamb curry with tameya (35F), couscous (45F), beef or chicken brochettes (48F), stir fry vegetables (24F), ground vegetable balls with yoghurt sauce (21F). Desserts include date nut bars (20F).

Snacks:

CAFÉ DE LA BROUSSE
Refreshment hut by the water, opposite Adventure Isle.

CAPTAIN HOOK'S GALLEY
Small snack bar serving from the cannon bays of Captain Hook's Pirate Ship. Hook's ham and cheese sandwich (25F), Jolly Roger Macaroon (12F).

FANTASYLAND

Table-Service Restaurant:

AUBERGE DE CENDRILLON
Overall star rating: **
Dîner-à-deux: 350F–450F
We found this the most disappointing of the theme park restaurants. It looks pretty from the outside and inside there are candy-pink tablecloths, candles and wrought iron chandeliers, but the restaurant has little atmosphere.

The meal we had was bland and uninspiring. The starter was a tasteless plate of sliced smoked duck. Then we chose to try the scallops with saffron sauce (bland and rather cold) and grilled salmon (perfectly adequate). Other dishes on the menu include roast duckling in burgundy sauce, ham on the bone braised in cider and frog legs with garlic petals. Apart from the latter, we were disappointed not to smell a whiff of garlic as this is supposed to be the only restaurant in the theme park serving traditional French fare. Desserts include Magic Carriage Sundae.

If you do decide to try this restaurant, go there when it is warm and sit outside on the attractive terrace where Cinderella's carriage is parked.

Fast-Food Restaurants:

PIZZERIA BELLA NOTTE
Star rating: *****
This is a prime example of how beautifully designed the Disney fast-food restaurants are. When you first walk in, it looks like a table-service Italian restaurant with pitchers of grapes on the walls, wine barrels on the ceiling, Roman mosaic fountains and an open fire. It is actually run like a typical pizza take-away restaurant – you can carry your pizza off in a cardboard box.

There are plenty of tables inside and out to sit and eat your meal. Portions are small. Spaghetti Bolognese (24F) comprises a spoonful of mince with a ladleful of spaghetti, but it tastes good and it leaves you free to "graze" round the other restaurants during the day! Pizzas (24F) are Mickey-shaped. Other dishes include lasagne (30F), garlic bread (10F) and tiramisu (28F).

AU CHALET DE LA MARIONNETTE
Star rating: *

One of our least favourite of the fast-food restaurants, as the limp looking food displayed in the cabinet here is such a turn-off. Dishes include roast chicken and chips (41F), burger and chips (28F), frankfurter and chips (28F) and chicken salad (32F). Desserts include apple or berry strudel (25F) and Black Forest cup (23F).

TOAD HALL RESTAURANT
Star rating: ****

Stop for an English lunch in Toady's old baronial home complete with Toad wallpaper, vaulted ceilings, leather chairs, draped velvet curtains, stained-glass windows and framed portraits of *Wind in the Willow* characters. Menu includes fish and chips (29F), roast beef sandwich with chips (36F), ploughman's (36F) and chicken and vegetable pie (32F). Desserts include trifle (16F) and fruit pie (12F).

Snacks:

MARCH HARE REFRESHMENTS
Outdoor café serving punch (11F), soft drinks and Unbirthday (vanilla and chocolate) cake.

FANTASIA GELATI
Ice-cream parlour next door to the Pizzeria Bella Notte, with unusual selection of flavours. 12F for one scoop.

THE OLD MILL
Outdoor café serving frozen yoghurt (16F), apple and macaroon tart (13F), fruit of the forest pie (12F) and yoghurt drinks (12F). Big queues on sunny days.

DISCOVERYLAND

Fast-Food Restaurants:

CAFÉ DES VISIONNAIRES
Star rating: ***
Futuristic restaurant serving couscous (38F), paella (42F), jumbo shrimp salad (36F) or chicken salad (32F). Desserts include chocolate mousse (5F), frozen yoghurt (16F) and apple tart (12F). Tables inside and out. Located next to the Discoveryland lake, this is a good place to sit and watch what is going on at Le Théâtre du Château.

CAFÉ HYPERION
Star rating: *****
An enormous tiered table and chairs self-service restaurant with a high-tech interior, painted in lime green and burnt orange. Teenagers will love the futuristic disco setting with muted disco music in the background and laser beams over the dance floor. The giant video screens occasionally show pop videos. Disco with flashing lights and loud music at night. Food includes grilled chicken, pastrami, smoked ham, smoked beef or tuna club sandwiches (20F–30F). Also chicken salad (36F), jumbo shrimp salad (32F) and frozen yoghurt (16F), chocolate mousse and apple pie (12F) for dessert.

FESTIVAL DISNEY

Again, we have awarded the restaurants a star rating (* to *****), based on atmosphere, service, quality of food and value for money. Dîner-à-deux prices are approximate guides to what you should expect to pay for three courses (without wine) à la carte.

Most of the restaurants also offer special set menus at reduced prices.

Despite their high prices, the Festival Disney restaurants get very busy, so it's best to book.

ANNETTE'S DINER
Star rating: **
Dîner-à-deux: 180F–250F (with a couple of beers)
1950s-style hamburger bar with a mint and peach colour scheme, formica tablecloths, plastic seats and a couple of cast members on roller skates. Standard burger fare at escalated prices. 65F for a basic burger (mine was overcooked and rather greasy) which comes with chips, served in a plastic tray. Guacamole burger (89F), Rock'n Roll burger (89F – with cheese and bacon). Also sandwiches and hot-dogs. Milkshakes (35F). Only come here if your kids are begging you for a burger.

CARNEGIE'S DELI
Star rating: ***
Dîner-à-deux: 150F–200F (for sandwich, dessert and coffee)
New York-style restaurant serving classic deli food such as lox and cream cheese bagels (49F), hot pastrami or corned beef sandwiches (45F), New York cheesecake (35F) and Manhattan Spice

Cake. Small restaurant with formica tables and food served in plastic basket trays, although many people queue for take-aways.

KEY WEST SEAFOOD
Star rating: ****
Dîner-à-deux: 400F–500F (without wine)

If you are going to splash out on a meal at Festival Disney, this is probably the most interesting and atmospheric of the restaurants and the prices are (fractionally) cheaper than at the Los Angeles Bar and Grill opposite.

The decor is very attractive – a long oyster bar down one side of the room, giant models of fish hanging from the ceiling and pictures of sailing craft on the wall. There are two circular dining-rooms overlooking the water, as well as a narrow connecting room to accommodate large groups of people on long tables.

Cast members are dressed in stripy t-shirts and white aprons. You are assigned a "Captain" (ours was Captain Claus) rather than a "waiter". The atmosphere is lively and raucous. Children will enjoy banging the table with the crab mallet!

Starters include chilled jumbo spiced shrimps (60F), Key West Chowder (50F) and the Sand Diggers bucket of mussels (65F). Main courses include broiled lobster with clam stuffing (260F), Fisherman's Stew (195F) and jumbo baked mussels with red crab sauce (140F). Desserts include Southern Pecan Pie, coconut cake with chocolate ice and sliced mango with melon sorbet.

LOS ANGELES BAR & GRILL

Star rating: ***

Dîner-à-deux: 500F–600F (without wine)

Located at the Lake Buena Vista entrance to Festival Disney, this is a bright, attractive Californian restaurant with lots of light coloured wood and hand-painted ceramic plates.

The restaurant downstairs is very expensive with starters such as house cured gravadlax, tuna sashimi or sautéed crabcakes at 85F. Main courses include roasted salmon with almond crust (140F) and grilled swordfish with papaya salsa (150F). Desserts include cappuccino crême brulée (45F) or lemon and thyme sorbet (40F). The restaurant also does pasta dishes from 90F and pizzas from 80F.

Upstairs is a bar and terrace where you can have a snack menu with wood oven pizzas from 45F.

THE STEAKHOUSE

Star rating: **

Dîner-à-deux: 600F–800F (without wine)

Considering that this is just a basic steakhouse, albeit with beautifully tender meat and a decor like a Chicago meat hanger, the prices are outrageous. Starters include Caesar salad (75F), jumbo shrimp cocktail (95F), spinach salad with hot bacon dressing (60F). Main courses include burger with cheddar cheese and bacon (125F), prime rib of beef (164F), sirloin steak (195F), t-bone (240F). Order a baked potato to go with your meat and they have the cheek to charge you 45F, 25F for spinach. Puddings include chocolate mousse (40F) and rice pudding (40F).

The restaurant has tables inside and outside.

FESTIVAL DISNEY BARS

SPORTS BAR
Large saloon bar with lifesize models of American sports heroes. Lively, young crowd. Tables inside and out. This was the only place in Euro Disney where we were served by a cast member who didn't speak any English. 18F for a half litre of Kronenbourg on draft. 20F for a glass of red wine. I objected to my Coca Cola (15F) being served in a paper cup. Snack food such as hot-dogs, turkey salad sandwiches and giant pretzels.

BILLY BOB'S BAR
Expensive country and western bar with live music every evening. Bottled beer 30F, Goldrush (pineapple and grapefruit juice) 50F. Limited selection of snack food served at tables upstairs – chilli (45F), chicken wings (40F), nachos with cheese sauce (30F).

The high price of beer means that younger people prefer to go to the Sports Bar opposite.

HOTEL RESTAURANTS

All the hotels have themed restaurants, licensed to serve alcohol. Prices in these are not usually more than in the restaurants in Festival Disney. Some of the hotel restaurants such as the Chuck Wagon Café are actually very good value.

Below is a brief round-up of hotel restaurants, highlighting the particularly good ones.

Hotel Disneyland

Café Fantasia: Fun Disney-themed café serving sandwiches and ice-creams.

Inventions: Recommended. Good restaurant for buffet meals of regional American cuisine, breakfast, lunch and dinner.

California Grill: Casual, elegant dining with Californian cuisine.

Hotel New York

Parkside Diner: New York-style diner with huge portions and potentially huge bills. Good for breakfast.

Club Manhattan Restaurant: The place to come for that special date. Romantic, elegant and expensive restaurant for dinner-dancing in Rainbow Room style. Jacket and tie required.

Newport Bay Club

Cape Cod: Recommended. Informal restaurant – good for pastas, pizzas and seafood.

The Yacht Club: Specialises in shellfish. Try their New England Clambake (steamed clams, potatoes, sausages, chicken, lobster and corn on the cob). Casual but smart – jackets required.

Sequoia Lodge

Beaver Creek Tavern: American barbecue grill with chicken, beef and rib specialities.

Hunter's Grill: Rotisserie specialising in marinated meats.

Hotel Cheyenne

Chuck Wagon Café: Recommended. Self-service styled like a Western town with nine different wagons selling speciality dishes. Good value for families. Large plate of barbecued food from the Range Rider particularly good value (89F). All food served cowboy-style on pewter plates and bowls.

Hotel Santa Fe

La Cantina: Self-service restaurant specialising in Tex-Mex dishes such as black bean soup and chilli con carni. Reasonably priced.

Camp Davy Crockett

Crockett's Tavern: Recommended. Small, clean self-service restaurant serving excellent hamburgers and other family fare, cooked fresh on a big grill in front of you. Large salad bar is also a treat. Reasonably priced.

CHAPTER EIGHT

THE UNOFFICIAL SHOPPING GUIDE

This chapter is for shopaholics who really want to savour the shopping at Euro Disney. It is also for people who hate shopping but want to know where the best things are, so that they can whizz round buying souvenirs and presents as quickly as possible.

All the shops at Euro Disney, in the theme park, in the hotels and in Festival Disney are reviewed, gift items are recommended and the best shops highlighted. For details about shopping in Paris, see page 233.

Not a place for bargains!

Euro Disney is certainly not a place to come for shopping bargains. One dad from Wimbledon, holidaying with his two young sons, said he spent £900 on souvenirs (mostly t-shirts!) for ten of his friends. In this chapter, however, we guide you round the best shops and suggest the better value presents and goods to buy.

Most of the shops stock overpriced Disney memorabilia. Disney and Mickey Mouse motifs are to be found on absolutely everything from golf clubs to lollipops. If you know where to look, however, you will also find some very high quality goods, and famous brand names such as Benetton, Levi's, Lalique, Osh Kosh and Crabtree & Evelyn.

There is no point bargain-hunting in Euro Disney as prices are standardised and you will pay the same for a Mickey hat whichever shop you buy it in.

A shopping paradise for children

All the shops at Euro Disney are themed and goods are beautifully displayed, a big temptation for children and a potential nightmare for the parents! By following the guidelines in this chapter, you will see which shops are really worth visiting so that you can promise to take the children to specific ones at the end rather than dashing into all of them and then having to deal with screaming tantrums when you won't leave with half the stock.

Pleasures of hassle-free shopping

One of the nice parts about shopping in Euro Disney is that you are under no pressure to buy and "cast members" never disturb you from browsing, even in the more expensive shops.

Best times to shop
If you are only there for a day, you will probably want to leave the shopping until the end of the day. The shops do get very busy at about 6pm, so you may want to wait until a bit later, just before the park closes. On longer stays, a good time to shop is first thing in the morning as the shops are usually quiet then. There are coin-operated lockers where you can leave small purchases underneath Main Street USA station. Bulkier items can be checked in with a cast member at Guest Storage.

Credit cards and travellers' cheques
You should be able to pay by American Express, Eurocard, Master Card, Visa or Carte Bleue at nearly all the Euro Disney shops. You can pay by travellers' cheques at the Disney hotels and at Festival Disney, but they are not accepted in the theme park.

TOP OF THE SHOPS

Here is our personal selection of the best and most interesting shops in Euro Disney.

Le Coffre du Capitaine (Adventureland) – Presents with a pirates theme.

Storybook Store (Main Street USA) – Books and audio cassettes of favourite Disney stories available in several European languages.

Tobias Norton (Frontierland) – High-quality Wild West souvenirs.

Star Traders (Discoveryland) – Presents with a *Star Wars* theme.

La Chaumière des Sept Nains (Fantasyland) – The place to come for children's Disney fancy dress outfits, particularly good for little girls.

La Boutique du Château (Fantasyland) – Specialist Christmas shop with trees and decorations.

Harringtons (Main Street USA) – Elegant shop for fine china, porcelain, Lalique glass and quality gifts.

Harmony Barber Shop (Main Street USA) – A chance to have an old-time shave and haircut.

Disney Clothiers Ltd – Good quality Disney clothing in beautifully designed shop.

Adventureland Bazaar – Fun and atmospheric place to browse.

La Confiserie des Trois Fées (Fantasyland) – If your children insist on going into one of the sweet shops, take them to this delightful little shop where there are floating fairies in the chimney breast.

Buffalo Trading Company (Festival Disney) – Presents with a Wild West theme.

Hollywood Pictures (Festival Disney) – Glitzy disco gear and glam clothing for teenagers.

SHOP REVIEWS

Like the rides and attractions, the shops have been graded (* to *****) and reviewed land by land, in a clockwise direction, starting in Main Street USA.

MAIN STREET USA

Main Street USA is a shopaholics' paradise, although many of the shops stock similar merchandise. There are two big shopping arcades, good places to browse if the weather is bad.

The quietest time to shop is in the morning, the busiest at the end of the day.

The shops have been reviewed in a clockwise direction, starting with Plaza West Arcade.

Plaza West Boutique
Star rating: *
A very ordinary Disney shop, this sells general merchandise and souvenirs. Most of the goods here you will also find elsewhere. If it looks like it is going to rain, it would be a good idea to buy your Mickey poncho now before you start touring the park. Other goods include Mickey ears, Minnie headband ears, souvenir mugs and sunglasses.

Storybook Store
Star rating: ****
Don't be fooled by the dusty facsimile books in the windows of this shop as inside it is all Disney books and music cassettes. You should find your

favourite story here, with editions in several languages. Despite being advertised as "books and records" there are no records, only cassettes and compact discs. While you are browsing through the books, look up above at the Disney characters unloading dusty tomes from the shelves. Tigger is waiting at a counter at the exit to stamp your purchase. Merchandise includes Ladybird books, Walt Disney's biography, Mickey's Wipe Clean Activity Book and Disney Souvenir Cassettes.

Liberty Arcade (Emporium)
Star rating: ****
This is an excellent spot to come if it rains. As well as going to the shops you can wander through the arcade to look at the Statue of Liberty Tableau and find out more about the French-American alliance in making Lady Liberty a symbol of freedom to the world.

The arcade houses the EMPORIUM, a turn-of-of-the-century department store with a beautiful domed stained-glass ceiling. In the store you will find some useful items such as a disposable flash camera with film in case you have forgotten your camera, and all sorts of clothing and presents for the whole family from baby to granny. Goods include cotton Minnie Mouse dresses, Donald Duck braces, Mickey rucksacks, Minnie Mouse slippers, Dumbo teapots, Euro Disney car stickers, wooden Mickey Mouse chopping boards, denim jackets with Mickey Mouse embroidered on the back, and black cotton polos with Mickey Mouse motifs.

As you walk through the department store you come to –

The Toy Chest which stocks a huge range of cuddly toys and games. Some of these, such as a small plastic Donald Duck on a skateboard (140F), are very overpriced.

Bixby Brothers, also part of the Emporium, sells perfumed goods by Crabtree & Evelyn and Woods of Windsor, as well as floral baskets, straw bonnets, Disney bow ties, socks and garish ties.

Harmony Barber Shop
Star rating: ****
If you rushed out of bed and forgot to shave, you can stop off at this corner shop for an old-fashioned shave (90F) or haircut (76F). The shop also sells shaving mugs and nostalgic shaving items.

Glass Fantasies
Star rating: ***
Here you can watch a glass-blower creating knitted glass fantasies such as Sleeping Beauty's Castle, a mini Mickey Mouse and an amazingly ornate Cinderella's carriage.

Disney & Co
Star rating: ***
The most original feature of this shop is the fairground theme decor with its distorted mirrors and colourful hot-air balloon. The goods on sale are similar to what you find in other shops. Dumbo baby bottles are fun for junior members of the family.

Discovery Arcade

This is located on the opposite side of Main Street to Liberty Arcade and is inspired by European inventors/writers Jules Verne and H. G. Wells. It features a host of curious inventions dating from the Industrial Revolution of the 1880s. If you are in need of shelter you can walk through the arcade and look at display cabinets of olde-worlde household items, toys and clothing. You can also sit in the arcade with a coffee or ice-cream bought from the arcade side of the Main Street cafés.

Harrington's Fine China and Porcelains
Star rating: *****

If you enter this shop from the arcade, you may think that all it sells is cheap china Disney souvenirs. The best merchandise is on the Main Street side of this elegant shop, with its stained-glass domed ceilings and ornate chandeliers and gilt pillars. The prices of some of the goods may knock you back – 20,000F for a porcelain tableau of Snow White and the Seven Dwarfs, 3,500F for a Pinocchio puppet! More reasonable gifts are available. Stocks Lladro, Royal Albert bone china and Lalique glass.

Main Street Motors
Star rating: ****

Small antique car showroom where you can actually buy a Harley Davison motorbike or vintage car.

Disney Clothiers Ltd
Star rating: *****

The place to come for quality but expensive Disney

clothing – a beautifully embroidered Pooh Bear t-shirt costs 1,125F. Elegant decor styled like an old drawing-room with rich thick carpet, piano and tailor's dummy. Clothing for all ages, including fancy dress outfits for children ("Alice" robes, Snow White dresses etc).

Boardwalk Candy Palace
Star rating: ***
Atlantic City sweet palace with marble floor and pretty decor. The place to buy giant lollies, Disney confectionery, chocolate and homemade cream butter fudge. You can watch the fudge being made on the premises.

Town Square Photography
Star rating: *
Old-fashioned photographic shop selling films, cameras and accessories. Don't make the mistake of getting your photos developed here as it is very overpriced. A 36-picture film would cost 168.20F to develop! Cameras can be rented for 50F per day (plus 500F deposit). Video cameras can be rented for 300F per day (plus 5,000F deposit).

Silhouette Artist
Star rating: *
Inside Town Square Photography. Paper cut-out silhouettes. 60F for the silhouette plus 60F to frame.

Ribbons & Bows Hat Shop
Star rating: **
Pretty Victorian milliner's shop with candy-pink wallpaper and pink velvet drapes. Disappointingly

there are no old-fashioned ribbons for sale, only touristy hats. One item worth purchasing in this shop rather than anywhere else is a Mickey Ears Hat (25F) as they will embroider your child's name on this for free.

FRONTIERLAND

Thunder Mesa Mercantile Building
Star rating: *****
Three high-quality Wild West shops housed under one roof. **Tobias Norton & Sons** stocks leather items, cowboy hats and gifts such as patchwork quilts, pewter plates and jugs. **Bonanza Outfitters** sells Wild West clothing such as suede waistcoats, Wild West t-shirts, buffalo button covers and bootlace ties. Also sells Indian-style goods such as headbands (fun for the kids) and chief headdresses. **Eureka Mining Supplies** sells Wild West toys (gun and holster sets), model cowboys, western finger puppets and food gifts such as Indian popcorn, spicy nuts and salsa in jars.

Pueblo Trading Post
Star rating: **
Small shop selling American Indian crafts. Pottery, wood carvings, glass, wall-hangings. Look out for the *American Indian Cooking and Herblore Book* (30F) which includes a recipe for Squirrel Stew!

Woodcarver's Workshop
Star rating: *
Traditional Indian carvings of animals and Red Indian heads. Will carve your name for 130F.

ADVENTURELAND SHOPS

Trader Sam's Jungle Boutique
Star rating: ***
Pagoda-style thatched cabin, evoking the style of a jungle explorer selling goods such as jungle t-shirts, binoculars and compasses.

Adventureland Bazaar
Star rating: *****
This exotic bazaar is fun to browse in, although if you have ever shopped in these eastern countries, prices in Euro Disney's bazaar will seem very high and there is no chance of bartering! The atmosphere, however, is great with lots of exotic murals, fountains and carved archways as well as impressive props such as the dusty Land Rover parked outside **La Girafe Curieuse** (which stocks safari clothing and accessories). **Le Chant des Tam-Tams** sells wicker baskets, pottery and drums. **Les Trésors de Schéhérazade** has an Arabian feel to it, with a giant camel walk-through and a selection of ornate clothing and exotic jewellery. **La Reine des Serpents** sells photographic books of eastern countries such as Morocco, Egypt and Turkey, pretty perfume bottles, ceramic bowls and unusual gifts for children such as pharaoh masks. **L'Echoppe d'Aladin** is good for ethnic jewellery.

Le Coffre du Capitaine
Star rating: *****
After riding on Pirates of the Caribbean, you can stop off here to buy your pirate's hat and pistol. Fun shop that stocks all sorts of pirate novelties, including stuffed parrots, wooden globes, toy tele-

scopes, rubber daggers and Captain's (plastic) hook.

FANTASYLAND

La Boutique du Château
Star rating: ****
Specialist Christmas shop with trees and decorations, Christmas cards, wrapping paper and advent calendars. Goods include knitted stockings, Snow White and the Seven Dwarfs Tree Set, Victorian-style Christmas decorations and potpourri.

Merlin L'Enchanteur
Star rating: **
Gift shop selling German glazed beer tankards, pottery dragons, tapestries, William Morris writing paper and a range of pewter mugs and plates.

La Confiserie des Trois Fées
Star rating: ****
Pretty little sweet shop with range of Disneyfied confectionery, teddy bear biscuits and giant lollies. Look out for the floating fairies in the chimney breast!

Le Chaumière des Sept Nains
Star rating: ****
Styled like a castle with suits of armour, this is a good place to buy Disney outfits for the kids, with Snow White dresses, Minnie dresses and Alice robes all at 295F. Other goods include Baby Minnie Mouse slippers, Pooh Bear rucksacks,

Mickey's pyjama cases and Disney sun specs. Also sells cuddly toys and baby clothes.

Sir Mickey's
Star rating: ***
This shop is divided into two sections. **La Ménagerie Du Royaume** stocks cuddly toys, ceramics and glassware, **Le Brave Petit Tailleur** sells Disney clothing (such as Goofy's baseball caps).

La Bottega di Geppetto
Star rating: ***
A "woodcarver's" shop selling wooden Pinocchios (from 80F), Pinocchio puppets (135F), animal building blocks and cuddly Jiminy Crickets and Pinocchios.

DISCOVERYLAND

Constellations
Star rating: *
On central display in this shop is Mickey in his flying machine. Goods comprise standard Disney gifts and cuddly toys.

Star Traders
Star rating: *****
Fun, futuristic-style shop selling Star Tours clothing, rubber *Star Wars* masks and laser guns.

FESTIVAL DISNEY

There are more themed boutiques at Festival Disney.

Bureau de Poste
Post office, telephones and bureau to change money.

The Disney Store
Star rating: **
Big store selling standard Disney merchandise such as mugs, toys, t-shirts, posters and books.

Team Mickey
Star rating: **
Euro Disney and Mickey motif on every imaginable sporting goods from tennis rackets to golf clubs. Golfing, tennis, baseball, American football and fitness merchandise.

Hollywood Pictures
Star rating: *****
Teenage girls will love this shop which is full of glamorous glitzy clothing, sequinned tops and baseball caps, black lycra dresses and gold lurex duffel bags.

Surf Shop
Star rating: **
Disney characters are on their surf boards at the back of this shop. Surf wear seems incongruous in this land-locked part of France but the shop stocks everything from surf shorts to beach towels and boogie boards.

Buffalo Trading Company
Star rating: *****
Wild West clothing and goods include Frontier-

land t-shirts, jewellery, stetsons, Davy Crockett hats and cowboy boots.

Streets of America
Star rating: ***
Themed goods from east to west coast. One of the best novelties is the photo service which enables you to have your picture on the cover of your chosen magazine (such as *Cosmopolitan, Musician, Rolling Stone, Ski*). Other goods include lacey dolls from New Orleans and Empire State Building ties.

DISNEY HOTELS

You will also find shops in the hotels. These sell the usual Disney merchandise at the same price as in the theme park, as well as some designer clothes and gifts fitting in with the particular theme of the hotel.

Disneyland Hotel: Galerie Mickey
Star rating: **
Victorian-style shop selling Disney merchandise and designer clothes by Lacoste, Théorème, Cacharel and Diapositive.

Hotel New York: Stock Exchange
Star rating: ****
The best hotel shop, as apart from Disney memorabilia, it stocks glitzy New York-style bags and t-shirts that teenagers will particularly like, plus stripey shirts for dad and designer clothes for mum.

Newport Bay Club: Bay Boutique
Star rating: ***
Clothing with a nautical theme, nautical books and gifts as well as designer clothes and Disney memorabilia.

Sequoia Lodge: Northwest Passage
Star rating: ***
National Park theme gifts and Disney memorabilia.

Hotel Cheyenne: General Store
Star rating: **
Wild West theme goods and clothing as well as Disney memorabilia.

Hotel Santa Fe: Trading Post
Star rating: *
Small shop selling Disney memorabilia and cheap-looking New Mexico theme goods.

Camp Davy Crockett: Alamo Trading Post
Star rating: **
Big store in the camp village selling Disney memorabilia plus food, drink and provisions for your cabin.

BEST BUYS

If you don't want to spend too much time shopping, the lists below should help direct you to some of the most interesting and best buys in the resort.

Suggested gifts for grown-ups

Clothing:
Disney hooded sweatshirt 250F (**Disney Clothiers Ltd:** Main Street USA)
Denim jacket, in Levi's style with Mickey Mouse embroidered on back 535F (**Emporium:** Main Street USA)
Black cotton polo neck with tiny Mickey motif 175F (**Emporium:** Main Street USA)
Disney Boxer shorts 110F (**Emporium:** Main Street USA)
Cowboy boots 1,100F (**Tobias Norton:** Frontierland)
Silver Star Tours jacket 250F (**Star Traders:** Discoveryland)
Jeans with suede pocket 450F (**Buffalo Trading Co:** Festival Disney)

Books:
Walt Disney's biography 175F (**Storybook Store:** Main Street USA)
Euro Disney souvenir book (paperback) 35F (**Emporium:** Main Street USA)

Novelties:
Dumbo teapot 375F (**Emporium:** Main Street USA)
Euro Disney car sticker 10F (**Emporium:** Main Street USA)
Disney cartoon ties 200F (**Bixby Brothers:** Main Street USA)
Buffalo button covers 30F each (**Bonanza Outfitters:** Frontierland)
Snow White and the Seven Dwarfs Christmas Tree

set 275F (**La Boutique du Château:** Fantasyland)
Star Wars Hologram Watch 350F (**Star Traders:** Discoveryland)
Cover Shot of You on Chosen Magazine 159F (**Streets of America:** Festival Disney)

Silly Gifts:
Mickey Mouse Hands 100F (**Toy Chest:** Main Street USA)
Mickey Mouse Slippers 195F (**Emporium:** Main Street USA)
American Indian Cooking and Herblore Book 30F – includes some disgusting-sounding recipes such as Squirrel Stew (**Pueblo Trading Post:** Frontierland)
Rubber *Star Wars* Mask 475F (**Star Traders:** Discoveryland)

Wildly extravagant:
Glass Cinderella's Carriage 2,600F (**Glass Fantasies:** Main Street USA)

Jewellery:
Ethnic earrings from 35F (**L'Echoppe d'Aladin:** Adventureland)
Wild West jewellery (**Buffalo Trading Co:** Festival Disney)

Suggested gifts for children

Toys:
Mickey 3-D Viewmaster 120F (**Toy Chest:** Main Street USA)

Pack of rubber Seven Dwarfs 125F (**Plaza West Boutique:** Main Street USA)

Cinderella Doll 250F (**Constellations:** Discoveryland)

8-sound laser gun 60F (**Star Traders:** Discoveryland)

Fancy dress:

Gun and holster set 135F (**Eureka Mining Supplies:** Frontierland)

Stetson 135F (**Tobias Norton:** Frontierland)

Wild West finger puppets 55F (**Eureka Mining Supplies:** Frontierland)

Alice Robe 295F (**La Chaumière des Sept Nains:** Fantasyland)

Snow White cotton dress 295F (**Disney Clothiers Ltd:** Main Street USA)

Pirate's hat 60F (**Le Coffre du Capitaine:** Adventureland)

Toy telescope 20F (**Le Coffre du Capitaine:** Adventureland)

Captain's (plastic) hooks 20F (**Le Coffre du Capitaine:** Adventureland)

Davy Crockett Hat 55F (**Buffalo Trading Co:** Festival Disney)

Cute and cuddly:

Cuddly Dumbo 125F (**Plaza West Boutique:** Main Street USA)

Cuddly Dalmatian Pup 100F (**Toy Chest:** Main Street USA)

Cuddly Dwarf (One of Seven) 125F (**Toy Chest:** Main Street USA)

Cuddly Pinocchio 200F (**La Bottega di Geppetto:** Fantasyland)

Cuddly Pig 175F (**Constellations:** Discoveryland)

Wildly extravagant:
Giant cuddly Mickey Mouse 2,950F! (**Disney & Co:** Main Street USA)

Cheeky accessories:
Mickey Ears – available in most shops, but the most original are with your child's name embroidered 25F (**Hats and Ribbons:** Main Street USA)
Donald Duck sunglasses 40F (**Disney Clothiers Ltd:** Main Street USA)
Minnie Mouse Headband Ears 40F (**Plaza West Boutique:** Main Street USA)
Minnie Mouse Slippers 125F (**Emporium:** Main Street USA)
Goofy Baseball Caps 55F (**Sir Mickey's:** Fantasyland)
Mickey's Pyjama Case 225F (**La Chaumière des Sept Nains:** Fantasyland)

Exotic goods:
Pharoah Mask 22.50F (**La Reine des Serpents:** Adventureland)

Best for baby:
Dumbo Baby's Bottle 39F (**Disney & Co:** Main Street USA)
Play 'n Pop Disney characters 175F (**Toy Chest:** Main Street USA)
Baby's Feeding Cup 49F (**Sir Mickey's:** Fantasyland)

Fun for school:
Mickey's Wipe Clean Activity Book 32F (**Storybook Store:** Main Street USA)
Mickey rucksack 65F (**Emporium:** Main Street USA)
Disney school lunch box 85F (**Toy Chest:** Main Street USA)
Star Tours rucksack 125F (**Star Traders:** Discoveryland)

CHAPTER NINE

THE UNOFFICIAL ENTERTAINMENT GUIDE

There is certainly no shortage of entertainment at Euro Disney, and many of the best events are free and included in the price of your entrance ticket. In this chapter we review the entertainment in the park and in Festival Disney as well as highlighting the entertainment in the hotels.

ENTERTAINMENT IN THE PARK

There are all sorts of entertainment and shows inside the park. When you arrive, go to City Hall in Main Street and ask for a weekly entertainment programme ("programme des spectacles") and this will give you the times of all the shows you want to see.

Below are reviews of the main events, graded from * to ***** for their entertainment value.

The Disney Parade (La Parade Disney)
Entertainment rating: *****
Free.
Great fun for children (and adults of kindred spirit). Watch your favourite characters ride down Main Street on colourful floats accompanied by music taken from the films that made them famous.

Some of the best floats include Pinocchio with dancing puppets, the pirates dancing aboard Hook's ship, the *Jungle Book* characters, Little Mermaid blowing bubbles and Roger Rabbit bringing up the rear in a concertina cartoon car.

In order to get a good viewing spot, get there about half an hour before. If it is too crowded to sit on the kerbside, perch on the railing around Central Plaza, in front of Sleeping Beauty's castle. From here you will see the start of the Parade, before it advances down Main Street USA. Face away from the sun or you will have to squint. The marching band heralds the start of the Parade.

Main Street Electrical Parade
Entertainment rating: *****
Cost: Free.
Magical evening parade with over half a million twinkling lights. As with the Disney Parade, you need to get there about half an hour beforehand for a good viewing spot.

Some of the floats are really spectacular. Look out for Dumbo who showers himself with twinkly lights and the happy faces of the It's A Small World dolls. Big Ben brings up the rear.

Fantasia In The Sky
Entertainment rating: *****
Cost: Free.
This superb fireworks display bursts into vibrant colour over Sleeping Beauty's Castle after the Electrical Parade. Accompanied by music from the film *Fantasia*. A truly spectacular end to a day at Euro Disney.

C'est Magique
Entertainment rating: *****
Cost: Free.
Excellent show on Fantasy Festival Stage with Disney characters miming along to boppy tunes.

This fun, lively show is the ideal opportunity to rest for half an hour and watch your favourite Disney characters join a troupe of energetic dancers.

Make sure you find a seat at least 15 minutes before the advertised starting time or you'll have to stand at the back or sides.

Rock Shock (Videopolis: Discoveryland)
Entertainment rating: *
Cost: Free.
Don't bother watching this dreadful rock'n'roll dance revue. One to avoid.

Sleeping Beauty (Le Théâtre du Château, Fantasyland)
Entertainment rating: ***
Cost: Free.
Mini-musical comedy performed by dancers and Disney characters on the castle stage with a set like a children's pop-up book.

Lucky Nugget Show (Lucky Nugget Saloon, Frontierland)
Entertainment rating: ****
200F per adult (reduced price for children).
If you want some lively entertainment with dinner, this show is ideal. The plot is rather corny but the can-can dancers are colourful, the atmosphere lively and your children will enjoy clapping along during the pantomime-style chase scenes through the auditorium.

Families and groups of people are seated at tables near the stage. Couples and single people have bar seats – not very comfortable for a one and a half hour dinner show.

The food is simple but good quality – tortilla chips and dips to start, followed by a choice of prime rib of beef or barbecued chicken and spare ribs. The beef is the better choice. Dessert is apple pie and ice cream. Coffees and fruit drinks are included in the price of your ticket. There are several shows each day – you have to eat to attend.

Tickets are on sale from the Lucky Nugget box office on the day of performance.

Street entertainers
Entertainment rating: ***
Cost: Free.
Wherever you go in Euro Disney, there are street performers to entertain you and enhance the atmosphere of the themed land. Ones to watch out for include the Barber Shop Quartet (Main Street USA) and The Gunfighters on the roof of the Lucky Nugget Saloon (Frontierland).

A night out in Festival Disney

It is hard to believe that this ugly entertainment complex is part of Euro Disney as it has none of the style and imagination that you find in the park. The restaurants are overpriced, the shops adequate but no better than those in the park, and the whole atmosphere is soulless and dreary, particularly on a damp evening. The silver and metallic columns look as though they are a temporary fixture – but they are not!

In terms of entertainment, it is worth going to Festival Disney to see the superb Buffalo Bill's Wild West Show. Festival Disney is also licensed so you can go there for a drink. Below is a round-up of the entertainment on offer.

Hurricane's
Entertainment value: ***
Cost: 120F entrance (includes one free drink). Entrance free for hotel guests.
Smallish discotheque where young teenagers

drink giant turquoise cocktails and bop the night away to Madonna and other poppy tunes. Unpretentious holiday atmosphere at inflated prices. Drinks cost 90F.

Buffalo Bill's Wild West Show
Entertainment rating: *****
300F (200F for the under-12s).
Lively Wild West show and dinner, starring Annie Oakley, Buffalo Bill, 40 cowboys and Indians and more than 80 horses, buffalo and longhorn steer. The Red Indian scene is particularly spectacular with real buffalo being rounded up by the Indians. Great fun for all the family. Entrance fee includes dinner (good quality and lots of it), raucous entertainment and a straw cowboy hat.

There are two shows every night: 5.30pm and 8.30pm. You can make your reservation in person at Festival Disney, at City Hall (Main Street USA) or by phoning 60 45 71 00.

Billy Bob's Country Western Saloon
Entertainment value: **
Live country and western music at a bar where you pay 30F for a bottle of beer. Not usually that busy, as it's cheaper to drink in the Sports Bar (see page 148) opposite.

Babysitting

Never Land Club
If you want a night out without the children in tow, you can drop them off at this children's club where they will be entertained by conjurers, clowns and films. The only problem may be trying

to persuade them to come home! Works out cheaper than a babysitter in your hotel room if you only have one child. Minimum stay – 3 hours (120F). 40F per hour thereafter. Can also provide dinner for them (49F). Open 5pm–12 midnight. Caters for 3–10 year olds.

Entertainment in the Hotels

Character breakfasts (Hotels Disneyland, New York and Newport Bay)
Entertainment Rating: **
140F (105F for kids)
Buffet breakfast in top bracket hotels attended by Disney characters. Fun for little kids but don't expect a show or lots of characters. It's very laid back and during a typical hour's breakfast you will probably only see two or three characters.

Evenings in the Hotels

Each hotel offers live entertainment in their bars or restaurants.

Disneyland Hotel – Jazz band in Main Street Lounge.

Hotel New York – Big band music in Club Manhattan Room for dinner dancing.

Sequoia Lodge – Piano music in the Redwood Bar.

Newport Bay Club – Piano music in Fisherman's Wharf Bar.

Hotel Cheyenne – Country and western music in the Red Garter Saloon. Dancing at the Yellow Rose Dance Hall.

Hotel Santa Fe – Mexican musicians in La Cantina restaurant and in Rio Grande Bar.

Camp Davy Crockett – Storytelling and singing by the campfire in the village (summer only).

CHAPTER TEN

THE UNOFFICIAL GUIDED TOURS

As you can see from the last few chapters, there is much to see and do in Euro Disney. In this chapter we show you how to make the most of your stay by avoiding the worst of the queues and seeing all the best attractions in a set amount of time.

We have included detailed tours both for adults and for families with young children. If you only have a day, follow our Whirlwind Tours. If you stay longer follow our Two-day Tours. If you have toddlers, they are probably too young to follow a carefully timed tour so we have highlighted the top attractions for them where you can take things at a slower pace. Thrill-seeking teenagers can follow the adult tours or they may like to dash off on their own and do the most exciting rides and attractions that we recommend. We have even highlighted the top attractions for grandparents.

Please check times of parades and shows at City Hall (Main Street USA) as these vary throughout the season.

For budding David Baileys we have included a Photographic Tour, highlighting the park's best vantage points.

Finally, as the weather at Euro Disney is so unpredictable, we have included Tips for Touring in the Rain.

THE WHIRLWIND TOUR FOR ADULTS

This has been specially designed to enable you to see and do all the best rides and see the best attractions in one day, with minimal queuing.

8.45am. Arrive at gates, and buy your ticket.

8.55am. Walk up Main Street USA to queue at side entrance to Frontierland, by Casey's Corner.

9am. Walk quickly to **Big Thunder Mountain Railroad**. If you get there promptly, you should board the runaway mining train almost straight away (later in the day the queues are horrendous). This is the best "thrill" ride in Euro Disney – don't miss it!

9.15am. You now want to make your way as quickly as possible to **Discoveryland** at the other side of the park. Here you will find **Star Tours**, another very popular attraction, where queues quickly build up later in the day. This gives you a simulated six-minute trip into space in a *Star Wars* type adventure setting.

9.45am. Most people will still be lingering in Main Street USA, so now is the time to do the third most popular ride – **Pirates of the Caribbean** in **Adventureland**. This is a 12-minute indoor boat ride through pirate-invaded territory with some wonderfully hairy moments when your boat has to escape from cannonfire. Great fun!

10.15am. Walk over the precarious plank bridges

to explore **Adventure Isle** and then stop for a coffee at **Captain Hook's Galley** before climbing the **Swiss Family Robinson Treehouse**. This 90-foot tree is a prime example of Disney "imagineering" as it's entirely man-made, from its roots to its leaves, and all the treehouse rooms are packed with detail.

11am. Now's the time to book a table for dinner tonight (7.30pm-ish) as the two most atmospheric Disney restaurants are both here in Adventureland. On a hot balmy evening, it's nice to sit outside on the terrace of the **Explorer's Club** and sample exotic dishes such as baked fish in banana leaf or grilled young chicken in coconut sauce. For a romantic dîner-à-deux, book at **Blue Lagoon**, a subterranean restaurant where you can sit in a tropical moonlit setting and watch the boats from the **Pirates of the Caribbean** glide by.

11.15am. Leave Adventureland through the **Bazaar** (stop to shop if you have time and money). Head for the stunningly ornate **Sleeping Beauty's Castle** and see the wonderfully authentic dragon in the dungeon and the Disney tapestries and stained-glass windows in the gallery upstairs.

11.30am. Have a quick look round **Fantasyland** and see how the queues are building up! For a bit of a giggle, you may want a quick ride on the lavishly painted horses of **Launcelot's Carousel** or take to the skies with **Dumbo the Flying Elephant** (both designed with the under-sevens in mind). The queues are never too bad for the **Mad Hatter's Teacups**, a typical fairground ride which whirls you round and round in giant cups. Alternatively, if it's sunny, you can wander round **Alice's Curious Labyrinth**, a maze complex leading to the **Queen of Hearts' Castle**. The best ride in Fantasyland is **Peter Pan's Flight** but in the middle of the day the queues are usually too big, so wait to do this one in the evening.

12 noon. Take an early lunch at **Pizzeria Bella Notte** (self-service) and then go to **It's A Small World**, a leisurely indoor boat ride through a world of beautifully costumed singing and dancing dolls. A bit twee, but fun.

1pm. Return to **Discoveryland** to watch **Le Visionarium**, a 360-degree vision film about time travel starring Jeremy Irons and Gérard Depardieu. Afterwards go into **Videopolis** and play on the interactive CDs.

2pm. **Captain EO**-a 3D film starring a crew of cuddly animals, a robot and Michael Jackson as funky Captain EO. Afterwards take to the skies in **Orbitron**, a flying machine that is low on thrills but beautifully designed. Alternatively, drive round **Autopia** in an open-topped racing car – this ride is rather tame and only really fun for people who haven't yet passed their driving test.

2.55pm. Take your place at **Central Plaza** for the 3pm **Parade** of Disney characters.

3.30pm. Stop for coffee and cakes at **Cable Car Bake Shop** or an ice-cream at **Gibson Girl's Ice-Cream Parlour**. Then walk off the calories by returning to Frontierland and **Phantom Manor**. The latter is one of the most imaginative rides at Euro Disney: a chilling journey round the haunted house in a swivelling carriage – lots of fun!

4.30pm. Spend a little while wandering around Frontierland where there is always plenty to watch such as **cowboy shoot-outs**, the **Molly Brown Steamboat** and the screaming crowds on **Thunder Mountain**.

5pm. Take your seat at **C'est Magique** at the **Fantasy Festival Stage** in Fantasyland – Disney characters mime along to Disney's boppiest songs in a first-rate professional revue.

5.30pm. You now have a couple of hours before dinner to wander round at leisure, shop, do more rides, or just observe and soak in the atmosphere. If your legs are tired you may enjoy a rest aboard the **Euro Disney Railroad**, an old-fashioned train which slowly chugs its way round the perimeter of the park.

7.30pm. Dinner at **Blue Lagoon** or the **Explorer's Club**.

9pm. Time for a quick after-dinner stroll. Euro Disney is even more magical in the dark. Adventureland with its flaming torches and exotic bazaar and Main Street USA with all its intricately designed buildings lit up are particularly spectacular.

9.20pm. Find a good spot on Main Street to watch

the **Electrical Parade** (only at weekends and Bank Holidays).

10pm. Dash back to Fantasyland to do **Peter Pan's Flight**. Queues are normally horrendous for this kiddies' favourite, although most people will have gone home by this time.

THE TWO-DAY TOUR FOR ADULTS

With two days to spend, adults can enjoy a more leisurely tour of the attractions, and also have time to discover some of Euro Disney's Entertainment.

DAY ONE

8.45am. Arrive at the gates, and buy a two-day ticket.

8.55am. Walk up Main Street USA to queue at the right of the barrier leading into Central Plaza.

9am. Walk quickly through the fountain area of **Plaza Gardens** into Discoveryland, keeping the golden spheres of **Orbitron** on your right, and go straight into **Star Tours**. This is a simulated six-minute journey into space in a *Star Wars* setting. You should not have to queue at all – but this is a real stomach-churner, so make sure you haven't stuffed yourself at breakfast!

9.30am. While the early arrivals are still milling around Main Street USA, stroll over to the opposite end of the park to ride **Pirates of the Caribbean** in Adventureland. Expect to queue for only five to ten minutes at this early hour. The 12-minute indoor boat ride through pirate-invaded territory is deceptively calm at the outset, but there are plenty of thrills and comic scenes ahead as you follow the trail of havoc left by the wayward pirates.

10am. After all that early morning adventure, you deserve a refreshment. Try **Captain Hook's Galley**, where they serve drinks and snacks. You can then climb the adjacent **Swiss Family Robinson Treehouse**, a 90-foot tree entirely man-made, from its roots to its leaves. All the treehouse rooms are packed with detail and you have a great view of Adventureland from the top.

10.30am. You can now spend half an hour walking through the fabulously atmospheric **Adventureland Bazaar**, full of colourful clothes and bric-a-brac from exotic countries. Take time to watch the craftsmen at work and admire the exquisite mosaics. Later, book a table for dinner tonight (7.30pm) as the two most atmospheric Disney restaurants are both here in Adventureland. If it's hot, go for the terrace of the **Explorer's Club** and sample baked fish in banana leaf or grilled young chicken in coconut sauce. For romance under cover, book at **Blue Lagoon**, a subterranean restaurant where you can relax in the calm of perpetual moonlight while the boats from the Pirates of the Caribbean glide by.

11.15am. Leave Adventureland through the main entrance leading to Central Plaza and head for the stunningly ornate **Sleeping Beauty's Castle**. See the smoke-breathing dragon in the dungeon and the Disney tapestries and stained-glass windows in the gallery upstairs.

11.30am. Head into Fantasyland through the rear of the castle. Ignore for now the rides based on European tales (**Snow White, Pinocchio** and **Peter Pan**). Instead, savour the atmosphere of the most picturesque of the four Lands. If the queues are not off-putting, try a quick ride on the lavishly painted horses of **Launcelot's Carousel** or take to the skies with **Dumbo the Flying Elephant** (both designed with the under-sevens in mind). The queues are never too bad for the **Mad Hatter's Teacups**, a typical fairground ride which whirls you round and round in giant cups. Alternatively, if it's sunny, you can wander round **Alice's Curious Labyrinth**, a maze complex leading to the Queen of Heart's Castle.

1pm. Take a leisurely lunch at **Pizzeria Bella Notte** (self-service).

2pm. Return to Discoveryland to watch **Le Visionarium**, a 360-degree vision film about time travel starring Jeremy Irons and Gerard Depardieu. Afterwards go into **Videopolis** and play on the interactive CDs.

2.50pm. Take your place at **Central Plaza** for the 3pm **Parade** of Disney characters.

3.30pm. Stop for coffee and cakes at **Cable Car Bake Shop** or an ice-cream at **Gibson Girl's Ice-Cream Parlour**. Then walk off the calories by making for Frontierland, through the imposing fortress gates off Central Plaza. Don't be tempted yet by **Big Thunder Mountain** – the queues for the trains will be at their longest. Instead, head for **Phantom Manor**, one of the most imaginative rides at Euro Disney: a chilling journey round the haunted house in a swivelling carriage. Expect to queue for a while, but most of the waiting area is under cover and there's lots to watch below you.

4.30pm. Spend a little while wandering around Frontierland where there is always plenty to watch such as cowboy shoot-outs, the **Molly Brown Steamboat**, and the screaming crowds on **Thunder Mountain**. You'll have more time to explore tomorrow.

5pm. Take your seat at **C'est Magique** at the **Fantasy Festival Stage** in Fantasyland – Disney characters mime along to Disney's boppiest songs in a first-rate professional revue.

5.30pm. You now have a couple of hours before dinner to wander round at leisure, shop, do more rides, or just observe and soak in the atmosphere. If your legs are tired you may enjoy a rest aboard the **Euro Disney Railroad**, an old-fashioned train which slowly chugs its way round the perimeter of the park.

7.30pm. Dinner at **Blue Lagoon** or the **Explorer's Club**.

9pm. Time for a quick after-dinner stroll. Euro Disney is even more magical in the dark. Adventureland with its flaming torches and exotic bazaar and Main Street USA with all its intricately designed buildings lit up are particularly spectacular.

9.20pm. Find a good spot on Main Street to watch the **Electrical Parade** (only at weekends and Bank Holidays).

10pm. Wait around to watch the **fireworks** explode over Sleeping Beauty's Castle. These really are spectacular. Still got some energy? Leave the park and head for **Festival Disney**, where things only start livening up after dusk. If you're in the mood for a cocktail and the chance to boogie down, try **Hurricane's Disco**. If country music is more your scene, there are live bands at **Billy Bob's**, where you can join the crowd at the bar or enjoy a late meal at one of the tables. Don't overdo it, though – remember you have a full day tomorrow!

DAY TWO

8.45am. Arrive at the gates.

8.55am. Head up Main Street USA to Casey's Corner, turn left and wait at the side entrance to Frontierland.

9am. When the barrier is lifted, walk quickly through the tunnel leading to Frontierland, turn left at the **Lucky Nugget Saloon** and then right, towards the entrance to **Big Thunder Mountain**.

THE UNOFFICIAL GUIDED TOURS

If you get there promptly, you should board the runaway mining train almost straight away.

9.20am. Leave Frontierland through the fortress gates by the Lucky Nugget Saloon and walk across the south side of Central Plaza to Discoveryland. Head for **CinéMagique** and *Captain EO* – a 3D film starring a crew of cuddly animals, a robot and Michael Jackson as funky Captain EO. At this time of the day, there should be no queuing. Afterwards take to the skies in **Orbitron**, a flying machine that is low on thrills but beautifully designed. Best to leave **Autopia** in reserve for this afternoon – this ride in an open-topped racing car is rather tame and only really fun for people who haven't yet passed their driving test.

10am. Now is your chance to catch up on the rides you missed in Fantasyland yesterday. Queues are normally horrendous for **Peter Pan's Flight**, but at this early hour you should have to put up with no more than a 15-minute wait.

10.30am. Walk over to **It's A Small World**, an entrancing indoor boat ride through a world of beautifully costumed singing and dancing dolls. A bit twee, but fun.

11am. Time for a breather. If it's a hot day, sit down and have coffee and ice-cream at **Fantasia Gelati**. Alternatively, walk back to the other side of Fantasyland and have coffee at **Toad Hall** restaurant where you can sit inside or out.

11.30am. If the queues are not too big, have a quick

ride on **Pinocchio's Adventures** or **Snow White and the Seven Dwarfs**. The latter is more exciting.

11.50am. If you feel you've exhausted all Fantasyland has to offer, walk through into Adventureland to explore **Adventure Isle**, a children's playground of giant proportions. Taking **Captain Hook's Pirate Ship** as your starting point, explore the maze of tunnels, caves, swing bridges and underground waterfalls. Don't forget your camera.

12.15am. Time to plan ahead for this evening. We suggest you either spend the evening Wild West-style at **Buffalo Bill's Show** (6pm or 8.30pm) or have a more sophisticated dinner at the first-class American restaurant, **Walt's** in Main Street USA. If you choose the latter, now is the time to book. Bookings for **Buffalo Bill's Show** can be made at **City Hall** (Main Street USA) or at the box office in Festival Disney – in which direction you are now heading.

12.25pm. Leave the park for **Festival Disney** but don't forget to have your hand stamped for re-entry.

12.30pm. Spend a while exploring Festival Disney's shops, then have a beer at the Sports Bar before heading to **Carnegie's** for a New York-style sandwich.

1.30pm. If it's dry (and, ever better, if it's sunny), ease back into the action after lunch by heading back to Frontierland and joining the queue for the **Indian Birchbark Canoes**. This is a more energetic way of navigating the waterways around **Big Thunder Mountain** than by the paddle wheelers or keelboats – and you'll see more.

2.15pm. Take time to explore the parts of Frontierland that you haven't already seen. Try your shooting skill at the **Rustler Roundup Shootin' Gallery** for 10F a round. **Cottonwood Creek Ranch** will give you the atmosphere of a small farmholding, with real animals instead of the animatronic variety.

2.50pm. If you missed out on the **Parade** yesterday, take your place on **Central Plaza** for a grandstand view. Alternatively, this is the time to grab a seat aboard the kiddies' favourites in Fantasyland, while junior is propped up on Dad's shoulders watching the Parade.

3.30pm. Afternoon tea? Treat yourself to some Victorian elegance behind the velvet swagged curtains in **Plaza Gardens**, or at a pavement table outside if it's sunny.

4pm. Time to tear around the race track (well, you can always use your imagination!) aboard one of the futuristic racing cars at **Autopia** in Discoveryland. Or how about a final whizz through the air on **Orbitron**?

4.45pm. If you've reserved a seat for **Buffalo Bill's** six o'clock show, your day in the park is drawing to a close. You've got time to do some last-minute shopping or queue for perhaps one more favourite ride before heading out through the gates for the last time. (If you've booked for the later performance, why not head back to your hotel for a shower? Don't be tempted to eat, however – there will be plenty on your plate during the show.)

6pm **Buffalo Bill's Wild West Show**. Alternatively, stay in the park until the later show or your dinner at **Walt's**.

Hope you enjoyed yourself!

THE WHIRLWIND TOUR FOR FAMILIES WITH YOUNG CHILDREN

This one-day tour has been specially designed to cater for families with young children. The rides are particularly suitable for 4–7 year olds, although older children will also enjoy them. The tour centres mainly round **Fantasyland** as that is the best place for children of this age. If you have younger children in tow, see our suggested Top Rides and Attractions for Toddlers.

8.45am. Arrive at the gates, and buy your tickets. Children under 12 pay a reduced rate.

8.55am. Walk up Main Street USA to queue at Central Plaza, then head for the entrance to Fantasyland (just to the right of Sleeping Beauty's Castle).

9am. Walk quickly through Fantasyland to **Peter Pan's Flight**, avoiding the temptation to stop and

THE UNOFFICIAL GUIDED TOURS

look at any of the pretty buildings. Peter Pan's Flight is the most popular children's ride in Euro Disney so you want to do it early before the queues build up.

9.20am. Cross over to **Dumbo the Flying Elephant** for an outdoor flying trip.

9.30am. Enter the world of **Snow White and the Seven Dwarfs** in a short, indoor journey through the witch's territory. If you are with very young or nervous children, it is better to take them to **Pinocchio's Adventures** next door, a similar but less frightening ride.

9.40am. Walk over to **It's A Small World**, on the other side of Fantasyland. This is a wonderful ride for small children, an indoor boat journey through the countries of the world, represented by dancing, singing dolls in national costume. Before you exit, spend a few minutes looking round the village of model houses, with windows at all heights for the children to peer through.

10.15am. Time for a rest and drink at **The Old Mill**, stopping off at the toilets next to Pizzeria Bella Notte (opposite It's A Small World) if required!

10.45am. Brighten up your morning with a whirl on the **Mad Hatter's Teacups**, a classic fairground ride that spins you round and round in giant cups.

11.15am. Walk round **Alice's Curious Labyrinth**

to the **Queen of Hearts' Castle**. Listen out for the squeaks and whistles from the hedges and look for the Alice characters peering at you from corners. Parents will want to have their cameras ready as there are some excellent vantage points from the castle.

11.45am. Time for one more ride before lunch. Jump aboard one of the beautifully painted horses of **Lancelot's Carousel**.

12 noon. Lunch at **Toad Hall Restaurant**, an old English baronial-style home specialising in English dishes such as fish and chips.

1pm. Visit **Sleeping Beauty's Castle**, the central landmark of Fantasyland. Climb upstairs to see the tapestries and beautiful stained-glass windows. Don't forget to go downstairs too and see the dragon (very young children may be scared).

1.30pm. Have a look at some of the Fantasyland shops. If you want to buy your child a fancy dress costume, **La Chaumière des Sept Nains** is the place to go. Alternatively, go to **La Confiserie des Trois Fées**, a pretty sweet shop – look out for the fairies floating in the chimney.

2pm. Now's the time to decide about this evening's plans. The park is even more magical at night, so it is worth keeping the children up for a special treat. If you want entertainment with dinner, book a table at the **Lucky Nugget Saloon** in Frontierland. Alternatively, a window seat at **Walt's** in

Main Street is well positioned for the evening **Electrical Parade**.

2.40pm. Find a good spot for the **Disney Parade**. This will be one of the highlights of your child's day so it is worth getting there early for a kerbside seat at the Central Plaza end of Main Street.

3pm. **Disney Parade**.

3.30pm. Time for tea and cakes at **Cable Bake Shop** or an ice-cream at the Gibson Girl Ice-Cream Parlour in Main Street USA.

4pm. Walk down Main Street away from Sleeping Beauty's Castle, looking at any shops that catch your interest. If you want to buy your child a Mickey Mouse ears hat, the place to go is the **Ribbons & Bows Hat Shop** in Town Square as they will embroider your child's name on it for free.

4.30pm. All aboard the **Euro Disneyland Railroad** which chugs around the park and is a good opportunity to rest tired little feet. Get off at the first stop (Frontierland Depot), or if your children are enjoying the ride and rest, continue on the train and return to Main Street USA, and walk leisurely back down to Frontierland.

5.15pm. Visit **Cottonwood Creek Ranch** in Frontierland (it closes at dusk). Small children will enjoy the opportunity to stroke the livestock which roam freely in this little farm.

5.45pm. Take a walk round Frontierland,

watching the screaming crowds on **Thunder Mountain** and the boats and the canoes on the water. Look out for the cowboy shoot-out on top of the **Lucky Nugget Saloon**.

6pm. Continue round to **Phantom Manor**, the spooky house at the top of the hill (very young children may find this too scary).

7pm. Dinner at **Lucky Nugget Saloon** (NB show times may vary) or dinner at **Walt's** (Main Street USA).

8.30pm. Time for some last-minute shopping or to re-do any of the rides in Fantasyland that your children particularly enjoyed. Make sure you take your place in Main Street at 9.15pm for the 9.30pm **Electrical Parade**.

10pm. **Fantasia in the Sky**. Look up above Sleeping Beauty's Castle to see the most wonderful fireworks display.

THE TWO-DAY TOUR FOR FAMILIES WITH YOUNG CHILDREN

This more leisurely two-day tour has been specially designed to cater for families with young children. The rides are particularly suitable for 4–7 year olds, although older children will also enjoy them. If you have younger children in tow, see our suggested Top Rides and Attractions for Toddlers, below.

THE UNOFFICIAL GUIDED TOURS

DAY ONE

8.45am. Arrive at the gates and buy two-day passports for all the family (reduced rates for under-12s).

8.55am. Walk up Main Street USA to queue at Central Plaza, then head for the Fantasyland entrance to the right of Sleeping Beauty's Castle.

9am. Walk straight round to **Peter Pan's Flight** – a wonderful journey over the rooftops of London to Never Never Land. Later in the day, the queues are horrendous for this ride.

9.20am. Take to the skies with **Dumbo the Flying Elephant**.

9.30am. Go to **Snow White and the Seven Dwarfs** or **Pinocchio's Adventures** if you are with younger more nervous children. The Snow White ride is actually quite scary, focusing on the wicked witch scenes.

9.45am. Walk into Adventureland. Most people will still be lingering in Main Street USA, so now is the time to do the wonderful **Pirates of the Caribbean** indoor boat ride.

10.15am. Visit **Le Coffre du Capitaine**, a shop next door to Pirates of the Caribbean, that specialises in pirate wear and gimmicks for the children.

10.30am. Walk over the precarious plank bridges to **Adventure Isle**. This island is great fun for children to explore, with lots of tunnels, underground caves and a shuddering suspension bridge overlooking the wrecked galleon. For some good photographs, walk up to **Spyglass Hill** which has several good vantage points over Adventureland.

11am. Stop for a rest and refreshments at **Captain Hook's Galley**.

11.30am. Walk over to the south side of the island and climb the **Swiss Family Robinson Treehouse**, a 90-foot tree, totally man-made from its roots to its leaves.

12 noon. Now's the time to book dinner (7pm) for tonight. Your children may have spotted the **Blue Lagoon Restaurant**, which you pass through on the Pirates of the Caribbean. **The Explorer's Club** (also in Adventureland) is another very atmospheric place to eat.

12.15pm. Walk through to Frontierland and have lunch at the **Cowboy Cookout Barbecue**.

1.15pm. Digest your food by strolling over to **Cottonwood Creek Ranch** where young children will enjoy stroking the livestock which are allowed to roam free in this spotless little farm.

1.45pm. Time for some action! If it's a sunny day, the **Indian Birchbark Canoes** is a fun way to explore the **Rivers of the Wild West**. If the weather is not so good, you may prefer the shelter of the **Mark Twain** or **Molly Brown Steamboats**.

2.15pm. Take a leisurely stroll through Frontierland towards Central Plaza, taking in the Wild West atmosphere and watching all the goings on such as **Big Thunder Mountain Railroad** and the cowboy shoot-outs on top of the **Lucky Nugget Saloon**.

2.45pm. Find a good kerbside spot at Central Plaza for the Disney Parade.

3pm. **Disney Parade** – this will be one of the main highlights of your child's day.

3.30pm. Stop for tea at **Cable Car Bake Shop** or an ice-cream at The **Gibson Girl Ice-Cream Parlour**.

4pm. Spend some time looking at the shops in Main Street USA. Go to the **Ribbons & Hats** shop if you want to buy a Mickey Mouse ears hat with your child's name embroidered on it.

4.30pm. Take a ride back up Main Street USA to Central Plaza aboard one of the old-fashioned **Main Street Vehicles** such as the horse-drawn tram that departs from Town Square. Walk into Fantasyland again.

5pm. Take your seat for **C'est Magique** at the **Fantasy Festival Stage**. You and your children will love this lively first-rate professional revue in which Disney characters mime along to Disney's boppiest tunes.

5.30pm. Go for a late afternoon whirl on the **Mad Hatter's Teacups**.

5.45pm. You now have just over an hour to look at the shops, re-do some of your children's favourite rides or just walk around and take in the magical atmosphere.

7pm. Dinner at the **Explorer's Club** or the **Blue Lagoon Restaurant**.

8.30pm. Adventureland, with its flaming torches and ornate bazaar, is particularly exotic at night so it is a good place for a walk. If your children are still crying out for action, take them for a quick ride on **Lancelot's Carousel** in Fantasyland.

9.15pm. Find a good kerbside spot for this evening's Electrical Parade which starts at Central Plaza.

9.30pm. **Electrical Parade**.

10pm. Don't forget to look up at the skies for the wonderful **Fantasia firework display**.

DAY TWO

8.50am. As you have a two-day passport you should be able to walk straight into the park.

8.55pm. Start the day with a train ride round the park aboard the **Euro Disney Railroad**. Beat the queues by getting to the station platform early.

THE UNOFFICIAL GUIDED TOURS

9.20am. Arrive back at Main Street USA. Walk down Main Street USA, stopping to take photos and windowshop.

9.45am. Walk across Fantasyland to **It's A Small World**, a wonderful indoor boat ride, through the countries of the world, represented by pretty dancing, singing dolls in national costume. Stop to look around the model village of houses on your way out.

10.15am. Walk round to **Alice's Curious Labyrinth**. Tell your children to listen for squeaks and squeals and to look out for characters peering at them from behind the hedges. At the centre of the labyrinth is the Queen of Hearts' Castle, which has some excellent vantage points for taking photos.

10.45pm. Time for a drink at **March Hare Refreshments** or try a yoghurt drink at the Old Mill.

11am. Walk over to **Sleeping Beauty's Castle**. Look at the tapestries and stained glass windows upstairs and if your children are old and brave enough, take them down to the cellar where a dragon lurks.

11.30am. Time to decide about this evening's plans. If you want a fun night out, **Buffalo Bill's Wild West Show** (Festival Disney) is superb. There are two shows – 5.30pm and 8pm. You can make your reservation at **City Hall** (Main Street) or in person at the **Buffalo Bill** booking office in Festival Disney. Children will love this show which stars 40 cowboys and Indians and over 80 horses, buffalo and longhorn steer. If you want a good but not quite as spectacular show in the park, book at the **Lucky Nugget Saloon**, a Wild West pantomime dinner show with can-can dancers. Alternatively, you could have a good quiet meal at **Walt's** in Main Street. Whichever you choose, make your reservation now.

11.45am. Walk into the futuristic Discoveryland. Take to the skies in **Orbitron**, Discoveryland's version of Dumbo the Flying Elephant!

12 noon. Have lunch at **Café Hyperion**, the biggest restaurant in Euro Disney with a futuristic disco setting that the children will enjoy.

1pm. Look round the **Star Traders** shop which sells all sorts of *Star Wars* gifts and toys.

1.15pm. Older children and dads may be unable to resist trying **Star Tours**, a six-minute simulated journey into space. There is a height restriction for this and it is not really suitable for the under-sevens so one parent may want to wait with younger children in one of the cafés. Similarly, the 3-D film ***Captain EO*** is great fun for bigger children but the villainess may prove too much for little ones!

2pm. Walk back across the park to Frontierland, stopping off to take photos, look at shops or re-do any rides on your way.

2.45pm. Go to **Phantom Manor**, the spooky house

THE UNOFFICIAL GUIDED TOURS

on the top of the hill (very young children may find this too frightening and be happier to watch the Disney Parade again).

3.30pm. Take a trip round the **Rivers of the Far West** aboard the **River Rogue Keelboats**. Again, families may wish to split at this point with older children and one parent going off to try **Big Thunder Railroad**. There is a height restriction for this ride and the queues may be very big. If it looks too long, wait, come back and do this after dinner.

4pm. You will now have seen the best attractions in the park for families. Use the next hour or two before dinner to shop, re-do rides or catch up on any that you have missed. Hope you had fun!

5.30pm. **Buffalo Bill's Wild West Show**. You may be eating later if you booked at the **Lucky Nugget Saloon** or **Walt's**.

TOP TEN FOR TEENAGERS

Teenagers may want to follow the adult tours or else do their own thing, following the recommendations below.

1. Star Tours (Discoveryland)
2. *Captain EO* (Discoveryland)
3. Autopia (Discoveryland)
4. Big Thunder Mountain Railroad (Frontierland)
5. Phantom Manor (Frontierland)
6. Pirates of the Caribbean (Adventureland)
7. Sleeping Beauty's Castle (Fantasyland)

8. Mad Hatter's Teacups (Fantasyland)
9. The Electrical Parade (Main Street USA)
10. Buffalo Bill's Wild West Show (Festival Disney)

TOP TEN FOR TODDLERS

Toddlers will enjoy the parades and character events more than sophisticated rides. Don't be fooled by sweet-sounding names such as Snow White and the Seven Dwarfs – this is actually much too scary for toddlers!

Below are the best attractions for toddlers.

1. Euro Disneyland Railroad (Main Street USA)
2. Main Street Vehicles (Main Street USA)
3. Cottonwood Creek Ranch (Frontierland)
4. Lancelot's Carousel (Fantasyland)
5. Dumbo the Flying Elephant (Fantasyland)
6. It's A Small World (Fantasyland)
7. Pinocchio's Adventures (Fantasyland)
8. The Disney Parade (Main Street USA)
9. Character Breakfast (Hotel Disneyland, Hotel New York, Newport Bay Club)
10. C'est Magique (Fantasyland)

GREAT FOR GRANDPARENTS!

There is plenty to do and see for grandparents, although they may, of course, be restricted with a toddler or two in tow. The park is not as big as it looks on the map, but if your feet get tired you can always catch the train or one of the other vehicles down Main Street. Remember, feel free to sit down at any of the restaurant cafés, even if you are not eating or drinking.

1. Euro Disneyland Railroad (Main Street USA)
2. Mark Twain and Molly Brown Steamboats (Frontierland)
3. Phantom Manor (Frontierland)
4. Pirates of the Caribbean (Adventureland)
5. Sleeping Beauty's Castle (Fantasyland)
6. Peter Pan's Flight (Fantasyland)
7. It's A Small World (Fantasyland)
8. Le Visionarium (Discoveryland)
9. The Disney Parade (Main Street USA)
10. The Electrical Parade (Main Street USA)

THE PHOTOGRAPHER'S TOUR

You are not allowed to take flash shots on the interior rides. Cameras and video cameras can be hired at Town Square Photography in Main Street USA but resist the temptation of leaving undeveloped films there as the processing prices are ridiculously high.

Some of the more obvious vantage points in the park are marked with Kodak Photo Spot signs. Below is our personal selection of the top places to get a good shot. Although the guide is aimed at the stills photographer, the vantage points suggested are obviously just as useful for the video enthusiast.

1. **Main Street USA**: For a general view, looking towards Sleeping Beauty's Castle, perch on the bandstand in Town Square. Watch for the Disney characters while in this area – Mickey, Minnie

and Donald can be found greeting arrivals filing through the turnstiles. Don't be afraid to shout and wave to attract their attention – they've made a career out of posing for the camera, after all! The façades in Main Street are all worth photographing, in particular the Market House Delicatessen and the Gibson Girl Ice-Cream Parlour. Try to get one of the passing veteran cars into the frame for added atmosphere. If you're photographing people there are usually some parked vehicles ideal for posing beside – or inside!

2. **Sleeping Beauty's Castle**: Avoid standing in front of the main entrance for your portrait shot – you'll end up with a frame full of people's backs! Instead, step round to the left side of the castle (next to Adventureland), where you'll have a wonderful view of the castle rising above the grassy embankment, and with the reflected image in the moat below. Be careful not to chop off the highest turret! Inside the castle, walk up to the gallery and use your flash to capture the ornate ceiling. The pretty stained-glass windows are worth taking close-up, especially Sleeping Beauty receiving her princely kiss.

3. The best vantage point from which to photograph all the action in **Frontierland** (and there's a lot to capture in one frame) is from the Crypt behind Phantom Manor. Because it's at the top of a flight of steps, you can look down on the water below. If you're patient, you'll soon have a keelboat, paddle ship or a canoe sail into the frame, with Big Thunder Mountain in the background. A silhouette of Phantom Manor against a cloudy sky

from this point can look rather menacing, while the shoot-out outside the Lucky Nugget Saloon will provide you with lots of action shots (don't miss the bandits on the roof!). For picturesque scenes of turn-of-the-century life back at the ranch, take some shots of the duck pond outside the Cottonwood Creek Ranch, with the windmill in the background.

4. **Adventureland**: The Moroccan-style entrance to Adventureland is the most photogenic of the four which lead from Central Plaza, especially on a sunny day. With the palm trees and sandy embankments, you could easily be in North Africa! Inside, there are plenty of vantage points in the bazaar to take atmospheric pictures, although most opt for the area immediately beyond the entrance, by the abandoned Land Rover. Next location stop is Adventure Isle – climb up to the middle of the suspension bridge for great views of the wrecked galleon and of Captain Hook's Pirate Ship. There is also lots of atmosphere amidst the branches and leaves of the Swiss Family Robinson Treehouse.

5. **Fantasyland**: If you have children, this is the place you'll want to capture their excited faces as they try out the rides. The Mad Hatter's Teacups is ideal – colour and lots of room to manoeuvre inside the cups built for four. Dumbo is best to photograph from outside the railings while the youngsters whizz past you. Alternatively, take your camera with you on the ride for an elephant's eye view of one of the prettiest corners of Euro Disney. Elsewhere, the façade of Sir Mickey's shop,

with its giant curly beanstalk, makes a fun picture; Toad Hall is an elegant pastiche of an English baronial hall; and the Queen of Hearts' Castle inside the Labyrinth offers another vantage point from up high.

6. **Discoveryland**: The airship suspended above Videopolis is an impressive sight to capture, particularly if you can frame it against a blue sky. For a more futuristic image, there's the *Star Wars* craft, posed as if in mid-battle outside the entrance to Star Tours. Finally, Orbitron is the obvious landmark which begs to be photographed, from the ground or from one of the circling rocket ships.

TOURING IN THE RAIN

You must be prepared for rain when you book a holiday at Euro Disney, so take some waterproof clothing with you whatever time of year it is. If you do get caught short, you can buy plastic Mickey Mouse ponchos and umbrellas in hotel shops, in Festival Disney and in the park itself.

Below are some suggestions of good attractions to try in the rain.

Main Street USA
- Euro Disneyland Railroad (the sides are open so if the weather is very bad you won't get full protection!).
- Liberty Arcade (exhibits of the making of the Statue of Liberty as well as shops to explore).
- Discovery Arcade (exhibits of inventions as well as shops and cafés).

- Main Street Motors (small car showroom selling antique automobiles and bikes).

Frontierland
- Phantom Manor (house of spooks with most of the queuing under cover).
- Lucky Nugget Saloon (book for a dinner revue to keep you entertained and out of the rain).
- Thunder Mesa Mercantile Building (contains three shops selling high quality Wild West clothing and gifts).

Adventureland
- Pirates of the Caribbean (indoor boat ride).
- Adventureland Bazaar (series of interconnecting shops that are still, unfortunately, a little damp and cold on particularly bad days – only come here if you get caught in the rain in this area).

Fantasyland
- Sleeping Beauty's Castle.
- Snow White and the Seven Dwarfs.
- Pinocchio's Adventures.
- Peter Pan's Flight (but if the queues are very big you will have to wait in the rain).
- Mad Hatter's Teacups.
- Fantasy Festival Stage (excellent show called C'est Magique).
- It's A Small World.

Discoveryland
- Le Visionarium – 3-D film. Big queues may mean a short wait in the rain.
- Videopolis – good place to come in the rain.

Play on the interactive CDs or have a coffee and watch the dreadful "Rock Show", consoling yourself that you are at least warm and dry!
- Star Tours – most of the queuing area is indoors.
- Star Traders (interesting shop to browse in).

CHAPTER ELEVEN

Excursions

Although Euro Disney is a world in itself, it is always fun to explore the surrounding countryside. Below are a selection of day excursions plus a guide to the capital city of Paris, which is only 35–45 minutes away on the RER network.

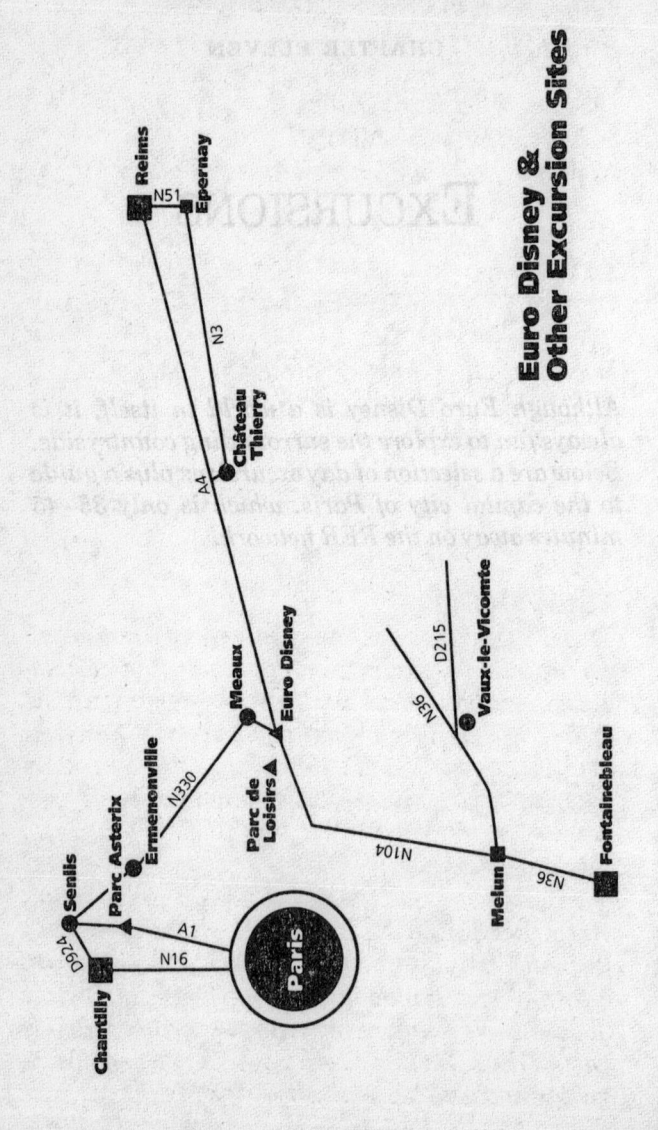

Euro Disney & Other Excursion Sites

EXCURSION ONE: CHAMPAGNE REGION

Distance from Euro Disney:
54 km to Château-Thierry
Approximately 100 km to Reims or Epernay

Directions from Euro Disney:
A4 to Reims
Or A4 to Château-Thierry and then N3 to Epernay

Why go to the Champagne region?
- To visit the champagne *maisons*.
- To escape into the countryside.
- To treat yourself to a night or two of luxury staying at the superb Hostellerie du Château (see page 58).

Description:
This is the only region in France where champagne can be made. Champagne is produced from a combination of white and black grapes grown from the chalky soil of this region and involves a double distillation process. The vineyards are owned by *maisons* who produce the champagne, or by *vignerons*, small cultivators, who sell the grapes to the bigger houses.

In a trip to the Champagne region you can visit one of the *maisons* to see how this luxurious drink is made. The two main Champagne cities are Epernay and Reims (pronounced Rance). It does not cost anything to visit the *maisons* although it is best to book. Most of them have English-speaking guides and will let you have a tasting. Make sure you wear warm clothing as it does get chilly down in the depths of the vaults.

One of the most famous champagne *maisons* is Moët et Chandon in Epernay, which has 28 km of subterranean vaults, while nearby is the Mercier *maison*. There is also a champagne museum in Epernay.

There are several champagne houses in Reims (the City of Coronations), as well as the beautiful 13th-century Nôtre Dame Cathedral, where 37 kings of France were crowned.

Further information
Moët & Chandon, 20 Avenue de Champagne, Epernay (Tel: 26 54 71 11)
Mercier, 70 Avenue de Champagne, Epernay (Tel: 26 54 75 26)
Pommery, 5 Place Général Gouraud, Reims (Tel: 26 61 62 63)
Veuve Clicquot, 1 Place des Droits-des-Hommes, Reims (Tel: 26 40 25 42)
Mumm, 34 Rue du Champ-de-Mars, Reims (26 49 59 70)

Tourist offices:
Reims: 2, Rue Guillaume-de-Machault (Tel: 26 47 25 69)
Epernay: 7, Ave de Champagne (Tel: 26 55 33 00)

EXCURSION TWO: CHANTILLY

Distance from Euro Disney:
About 50 km.

Directions from Euro Disney:
A4 east from Paris, exit Meaux, then N330 to Senlis and D924 on to Chantilly

Why go to Chantilly?
- Chantilly Château.
- Horse racing.
- Horse and pony museum.
- Shopping.
- Walks in the forest.

Description:
After visiting Sleeping Beauty's Castle (Le Château de la Belle au Bois Dormant), why not drive out to the French countryside and see a real French château in Chantilly? This magical castle is reached across a moat guarded by two beautiful bronze hunting hounds.

The Chantilly estate dates back to the tenth century and was bought in the late 14th century by the Chancellor of France, Pierre d'Orgemont, who together with his son, Amaury, rebuilt the castle into a fortress with seven towers. Amaury never had children, so when he died the estate passed to his sister Marguerite, wife of Philippe de Montmorency. It was the Montmorency family and the Condés (also related to the Orgemonts through marriage) who had the most influence on the Chantilly estate.

Constable Anne de Montmorency was a very wealthy man (at one time he owned over a hundred castles and estates) and he commissioned Pierre Champiges to renovate the château in the French Renaissance style. The Constable also had the

Petit Château ("little castle") built – this was originally separated from the main château by water.

Unfortunately, the main castle was destroyed during the Revolution, and was not restored until the late 19th century when it was owned by the Duke of Aumale (the fourth son of King Louis-Philippe). The Duke insisted that the architecture of the château should not be modified in any way and left his art collections and the estate to the Institut de France. The castle is now a museum housing his collections. The Petit Château still stands and now houses the Duke of Aumale's library. However, only two of the seven chapels which were built by Constable Anne de Montmorency are still standing today.

The Condé museum was created by the Duke of Aumale and now houses hundreds of paintings and several thousand drawings. These include some Raphaels and a Fillipino Lippi and there are also miniatures from a 15th-century *Book of Hours* which has been attributed to Jean Fouquet.

The highlight of the museum is *Les Très Riches Heures du Duc du Berry*, the most famous of all *Books of Hours*, housed in the library, the Cabinet des Livres. You can only see this with a guide.

There are plenty of other things to see and do in Chantilly. One, five minutes walk away, is the Musée Vivant du Cheval (Living Horse Museum), housed in the giant stables, built in 1719 by Louis-Henri de Bourbon, the seventh Prince of Condé, who believed that he would be reincarnated as a horse and so was obviously keen to provide good accommodation for his future relatives! The stables housed 240 horses and up to 500 hounds. The Musée Vivant du Cheval was founded in 1982 by a riding master called Yves Bienaime. This private museum comprises a series of rooms, each with its own educational and horse-related theme, including one devoted to the blacksmith's trade, a veterinary's operating room, children's horse toys and tack rooms. If you are not a horse buff, these exhibits are rather dull and you will probably prefer wandering around the stalls and looking at the beautiful horses, which you will later see performing in a dressage-based demonstration in the central arena. In this equine display, talented riders show off the skills of Andalusian and Portuguese horses, similar to those ridden by the Princes in the 18th century when the stables were built. During the Christmas holidays, there is a particularly lavish show which is great fun for children.

If you are interested in a bit of a flutter, there is also a racecourse in Chantilly. Alternatively, take a walk around the town itself, which is full of chic boutiques and restaurants. Le Restaurant du Château in Rue de Connetable is a lively, atmospheric place to stop for a three-course lunch, which you can then walk off in the nearby woods of Chantilly.

Further Information:
Office de Tourisme, 23, Avenue du Maréchal, Chantilly (Tel: 44 57 08 58)

EXCURSION THREE: FONTAINEBLEAU

Distance from Euro Disney:
63 km

Directions from Euro Disney:
A4 towards Paris, then exit Emerainville/Melun (N104). Drive to Melun, then take N6 to Fontainebleau.

Why go to Fontainebleau?
- The château of Fontainebleau.
- The arty village of Barbizon.
- Walking, cycling, climbing or horseriding in the forest.
- Peace and quiet.
- Vaux-le-Vicomte (*see Excursion Seven*).

Description:
After an action-packed stay at Euro Disney, Fontainebleau is the ideal place to relax and unwind either for a day trip or extended part of your holiday.

The town of Fontainebleau is very attractive and full of restaurants, Parisian-style cafés and chic boutiques. Personally, I prefer to stay a little more off the beaten track, at the nearby village of Samois-sur-Seine, where there is a very good and reasonably priced hotel called Hostellerie du Country Club (*see page 57*) on the river.

Fontainebleau is dominated by the huge, sprawling château with Disney-like façades. Originally a hunting lodge, this dates back to the 12th century, although over the years many of the great kings seem to have made their mark on it. It was particularly influenced by François I, who used Italian renaissance craftsmen to work on the interiors of the château in the 16th century. The Gallery of François I is a fine example of renaissance art by the Italian artist Rosso. Napoleon

Bonaparte also had a big influence on the château and actually signed his abdication there on 6 April, 1814. Two weeks later, on 20 April, 1814, Napoleon bade farewell to his troops at the top of the sweeping horseshoe staircase. The château now houses the Napoleon I Museum which occupies a series of rooms on the ground level and on the first floor of the Louis XV wing.

The gardens of the château can also be visited and are very beautiful. The Garden of Diana is named after the famous fountain statue of Diana hunting, although the original is now in the Louvre (the one in the garden is a bronze copy).

About five kilometres from Fountainebleau is the pretty but touristy village of Barbizon where landscape artists such as Jean-François Millet and Théodore Rousseau and writers such as George Sand found inspiration. There is one long main street, full of villas, restaurants and hotels, proudly bearing commemorative plaques of the artists who lived there.

The Ancienne Auberge du Père Ganne (Father Ganne's Old Inn) used to be a grocery run by Father Ganne, offering cheap lodgings for artists, and is now a museum showing how they lived and exhibiting some of their landscape paintings. Further along the high street is the old barn which Rousseau used as a studio, now converted into the Barbizon School Municipal Museum and housing work by Barbizon masters such as Rousseau, Dupré and Jacue and disciples of theirs such as Ortmans, Ciceri, Gassies, Chaigneau and de Penne. It will not take you long to tour this tiny museum. Afterwards you can stroll round the village looking at works by contemporary artists and crafts people, and stop for lunch in one of the many traditional village restaurants.

The Fontainebleu forest, once a royal hunting ground, is now frequented by rosy-cheeked walkers, cyclists, riders and climbers. The local riding school is at 29, Rue de l'Arbre Sec and provides tuition and trekking in the forest.

Further Information:
Tourist Office, 31, Place Napoléon Bonaparte (Tel: 64 22 25 68)

EXCURSION FOUR: PARC ASTERIX

Distance from Euro Disney:
40 km

Directions from Euro Disney:
A4 to Meaux, N330 to Ermenonville, then DN22 to the A1 (northbound, Lille direction). Parc Asterix is signposted just a few kilometres up the A1.

Stopping Off En Route:
If you are going to Parc Asterix with children, you won't have much time to spare, as it will take most of the day to explore the theme park. If you do want to combine half a day at Parc Asterix with a few hours sightseeing, stop off to see the cathedral at Meaux which dates back to the 12th century or visit the pretty village of Ermenonville to see the 18th-century château and park where Rousseau died and was later buried on an island in the lake. Rousseau's body is no longer there as he was moved to the Pantheon during the Revolution.

EXCURSIONS

Why go to Parc Asterix?
- To see the French alternative to Euro Disney.
- To experience French culture and history in theme park format.
- For roller-coaster and fairground-style rides that you will not find in Euro Disney.
- For a fun day for little children to explore Asterix village.

Description:
If Euro Disney has whetted your appetite for theme parks, Parc Asterix is only 30 minutes drive away, and well worth a visit, as it is so different from its American counterpart. The whole park, set in the heart of a 155-hectare forest, is based around the adventures of the French comic strip *Asterix*, which was created by two Frenchmen, René Goscinny and Albert Uderzo in the late 1950s.

The theme park opened in April 1989 and until Euro Disney, was the biggest in France, attracting over one million visitors each year. Smaller than Euro Disney, Parc Asterix does not have on-site hotels, so most visitors are day-trippers from Paris or other parts of France, although there are always staff on hand who speak English.

The opening of Euro Disney obviously throws a cloud over the future of this French theme park. "We were worried about Disney for the first year," a Parc Asterix representative admitted. "But then we are very different from Disney."

They certainly are like chalk and cheese. Parc Asterix is as French as Disney is American. If you are expecting the sophistication, slickness and high-tech animatronics of Disney, you will feel short-changed at Parc Asterix. The French park is cruder but charming, relying more on the humour of its street performers and side-shows and its offbeat education in the history of France with more of a fairground atmosphere than the American version. You don't find anything as stomach-churning at Euro Disney as the giant roller-coaster at Parc Asterix.

For those who are not familiar with Goscinny's and Uderzo's comic strip, Asterix is a brave little Gaul who always wins even in times of great adversity. The first thing you see when you pull up in the car park is the funny-looking little character perched on the top of a mountain. Asterix's main ally is roly-poly Obelix with his long red plaits.

Although René Goscinny died in the 1970s, Albert Uderzo has continued producing *Asterix* books on his own. The stories of Asterix are full of Latin names, jokes and puns, although both Goscinny and Uderzo claimed they didn't know any Latin at all and had to look it all up! *Asterix* is written in French but all the titles have been translated into English by Anthea and Derek Hockridge, so if you are planning a trip to the theme park, you or your children may enjoy reading a book or two first to prepare you for the atmosphere and spirit of the Asterix world.

Like Euro Disney, Parc Asterix is arranged into different thematic sections, the highlights of which are described below. If you want to see and experience all the sections at leisure, you really need a whole day. Beer and wine are sold in Parc Asterix (alcohol is banned at Euro Disney).

Via Antiqua

This is the first section you walk through after entering the gates. Asterix and Obelix are often waiting here to greet you and are happy to offer a hug and pose for photos! Piped medieval music sets the atmosphere as you wander down the main street, lined with shops and snack bars. You'll immediately sample the Asterix humour – the "Servix" station with its unleaded hay pumps and the photo shop, "Touthandeclick".

All the practical services are found in this area, including an information centre, a place where pushchairs can be hired and coats and luggage checked in, the Credit Latin where you can change currency, a First-Aid Centre and an office to go to if you have lost your children.

The Roman City

Once you get to the top of Via Antiqua you enter the Roman City. Straight ahead of you is the Gladiators' Arena, immediately transporting you into the ancient world of gladiators and barbarians. Twice a day, the Olympic Games are held in this uncovered arena, and is an attraction not to be missed. Watch where you sit during this 30-minute show! I had the shock of my life when "something" jumped out from under my seat (you'll see what I mean!).

To the left of the amphitheatre is the Grand Carousel, a Roman version of the traditional merry-go-round, fun for little children and adults like myself who still enjoy the magical sensation of gliding round on a brightly painted horse.

You cannot go to ancient Rome without seeing a chariot race and this is depicted in fairground style with Ben Hur's Chariots, alias good old-fashioned bumper cars. Opposite this is one of the most popular attractions, the Descent of the Styx. Expect to queue for this ride, particularly in the heat of the summer when the thought of plummeting down the rapids in family-size giant rubber rings is most appealing. This is a tame but enjoyable ride, suitable for all ages.

Young children will enjoy the Petitbonum Camp, next to Ben Hur's Chariots. This is an adventure playground, made of wood logs for little Gauls to climb and slide around in.

If you are in need of lunch or a refreshing ice-cream, Caius Cepaderefus is a clean pizza restaurant in the Roman City area, where service is brisk. Alternatively, you can grab a snack at the fast-food restaurant Fastes de Rome.

The Asterix Village

If you have young children, this section is a must as it is such fun for them to run in and out of the 16 huts, designed by Albert Uderzo and built of stone, wood and thatch. All sorts of different scenes are depicted in these little dwellings. For example, in one you will find Asterix and Obelix having breakfast together, in another Falbala and Bonnemine are shopping. You can also watch a puppet show, or lean over and listen to the Magic Well.

You can continue your journey through the village by boat. This trip is called the Asterix Run, and although much less sophisticated than Disney's Pirates of the Caribbean, depicts a similar scene of combat in which the Gauls eventually triumph.

Before you leave this section, little children will

enjoy the Carute forest with its mini-village, mini roller-coaster and little train. Listen out for the bird songs (recorded!) in the forest.

The Great Lake

This depicts the charm of the Mediterranean and houses the largest (2,000 seats) dolphinarium in Europe. Regardless of my own reservations about keeping these beautiful animals in captivity, the show is rather slow-moving for young children, although there are some entertaining highlights such as the man who swims with the dolphins and the children from the audience who cross the water in a boat, towed by them. Two glossy black sea-lions also star in the show. This is always a popular attraction, so be prepared to queue.

For teenagers and thrillseekers, the most exciting ride at Parc Asterix is the Goudurix, at the far side of the lake. This is the largest roller-coaster in Europe and will loop you upside down no less than seven times, travelling at speeds of up to 75km per hour. Not for the faint-hearted!

Another ride for those wanting to experience the sensation of the lake rushing towards them is the Roman Galley, which is like a giant see-saw over the lake swinging you through 90 degrees.

Afterwards, if your stomach can handle a sit-down meal, the Arcimboldo is a bright, cheerful-looking restaurant, overlooking the lake. This has been designed out of giant colourful plastic fruit and specialises in grilled food. They also have a Junior menu for 40F (under-12s). If it is a hot day and you just want a sandwich, soft drink or ice-cream, there are snack places by the lake.

The Rue de Paris

From an educational point of view, this is the most interesting section as you experience different centuries of French history. You enter Paris over the drawbridge by the Great Lake. This leads you to the Medieval Square, where some fantastic acrobats, jugglers and tumblers perform. There is also a show called the Court of Miracles inspired by Victor Hugo's *The Hunchback of Notre Dame* and starring Esmeralda and Quasimodo. All the shows and films are in French so if you don't speak the language well, you miss out on a lot of the fun. Non-speakers should stick to the more visual shows such as the acrobats and jugglers.

As you enter inside this section, you come across all the shops depicting crafts of the 19th century. This is educational for children who can watch craftsmen demonstrate how the potter, basket-weaver, printer, cabinet-maker, weaver and sculptor used to work. This century is depicted with great vigour and vitality. You can stop to watch the Dances from the Belle Époque or see the Artist's Hotel which lights up to show the great men of the century such as Hugo, Moet, Offenbach, Toulouse-Lautrec and Gounod. If you want a souvenir of your visit, you can have your photo taken in period costume at Nicephore Beloizeau or visit Le Bonheur des Dames, a recreation of the first department store in Paris.

Young children will love the Animal Studio where they can be made-up as a superstar dog or cat. There is also a film about dogs and cats, all in French, but still fun for children who have pets at home. Alternatively, you can watch a 3-D film on nature in the Great Canadian North – although it falls far short of *Captain EO* at Euro Disney.

If you want to eat in this part of the park, you can dine under the big top at the Restaurant du Cirque.

Gergovie Square

If you want to end your day on an upbeat note, you can try the mini roller-coaster, The Trans Arverne, tame enough not to terrify Granny. Finally, if it's a hot day and you don't mind leaving the park a little wet, have a final ride on the Big Splash.

Attractions For Little Gauls

- The Big Merry-Go-Round (The Roman Citadel) – For all the fun of the fairground.
- Petitbonum Camp (The Roman Citadel) – Adventure playground.
- Gaul Huts (Asterix Village) – Run in and out of the world of Asterix.
- The Asterix Run (Asterix Village) – A boat trip through invaded France.
- The Little Train (Asterix Village) – For tiny tots.
- The Serpentine (Asterix Village) – Little big dipper.
- The Dolphinarium (The Great Lake) – Dolphin and sea-lion show.
- Les Petits Drakkars (The Great Lake) – Boats for little Vikings.
- The Little Swingchairs (The Great Lake) – For high fliers.
- Workshops (Rue de Paris) – Watch the craftsmen at work.

- The Little Carousel (Rue de Paris) – Wooden horses for little knights.
- Animal Studio (Rue de Paris) – Chance to be made-up into a superstar dog or cat.
- The Baby Bumper Chariots (Gergovie Square) – For baby Ben Hurs.
- The Trans-Arverne (Gergovie Square) – Tame roller-coaster for all the family.

Attractions For Thrill-Seekers
- Goudurix (The Great Lake) – Stomach-churning roller-coaster.
- The Roman Galley (The Great Lake) – For those who like their stomach in their mouth.
- Big Splash (La Place de Gergovie) – A guaranteed soaking!

Attractions For History Buffs
- Rue de Paris – This whole section traces ten centuries of French history.

Attractions Not To Be Missed
- The Gladiators' Arena (The Roman Citadel) – Entertaining warm-up for the Olympic Games.
- Down the Styx River (The Roman Citadel) – Fun water ride for all the family.
- Gaul Huts (Asterix Village) – Houses for Asterix and his friends.
- The Goudurix (The Great Lake) – Upside down view of the lake.
- Medieval Square (Rue de Paris) – Brilliant jugglers and acrobats.
- Dances from the Belle Epoque (Rue de Paris) – Flavour of Paris during that time.

EXCURSIONS

- The Big Splash (Gergovie Square) – Chance to cool down on a hot summer's day.

Further Information:
Entrance: 150F for adults; 105F for children under 12 (free for children under three)
Open from April to October.
Parc Asterix, Plailly (Tel: 44 62 32 10)

EXCURSION FIVE: PARC DE LOISIRS DE TORCY

Distance from Euro Disney:
8 km

Directions from Euro Disney:
A4 west towards Paris then exit A104 towards Torcy and follow signs to Parc de Loisirs.

Why go to Parc De Loisirs?
- For a day on the beach.
- For a picnic.
- To do some sports.

Description:
Parc de Loisirs is a 25-hectare lake with a wide range of sporting facilities including catamaran sailing, windsurfing, pony riding, canoeing, pedalos, mini-golf and a sandy beach with marked-out swimming area. You have to pay to drive in, so it is worth taking a picnic and spending an afternoon or whole day there.

Further Information:
Parc de Loisirs de Torcy, Marne-la-Vallée (Tel 64 80 58 75).

EXCURSION SIX: PARIS

Distance from Euro Disney:
32 km.

Directions from Euro Disney:
A4 into Paris via Porte de Bercy. As parking is a problem in the centre of the city, it is easier to take the RER train direct from Euro Disney into the centre of Paris.

Why go to Paris?
- To see one of the world's most beautiful cities.
- For sightseeing, museums, art and culture.
- To shop until you drop.
- For a romantic day out.

Description:
Euro Disney is only half an hour by car or train from Paris, so if you have a day to spare it is certainly worth touring this beautiful city. My personal advice is to leave your car at Euro Disney and take the train, as otherwise you could spend the whole day trying to find somewhere to park. The centre of Paris, where you will find most of the following attractions, is fairly compact, so you should be able to tour it all by foot or by using the highly efficient metro system.

There is so much to see and do in the French capital that it is hard to do it justice in one small section of a book. I have tried to group together different types of activities, so that you can easily plan your own itinerary before you go. Don't try to cram in too much in a day or you will end up exhausted – the art treasures of the Louvre, for example, could easily be a whole day excursion! When planning your day, try to choose attractions that are in a similar area or at least within walking distance. Travelling on foot is actually the best way to get the flavour of this wonderful city, so put your most comfortable shoes on and have a good day!

Shopaholics

If your trip to Euro Disney hasn't financially stripped you bare, Paris is one of the best cities in the world to shop, and even if money is tight it can be almost as much fun browsing and window shopping.

Haute Couture: If you are looking for the top of French designer fashion, go to Avenue Montaigne and Faubourg St-Honoré. In Avenue Montaigne (Champs-Elysées metro), you will find shops such as Karl Lagerfeld, Nina Ricci, Christian Dior, Louis Vuitton, Valentino and Cartier. In Faubourg St-Honoré (Madéleine metro) you will find Yves Saint Laurent, Lanvin, Hermès, Gucci, Chloë and Lacroix (for really outrageous and outrageously expensive outfits!).

Department Stores: For beautiful lingerie, designer clothes and fashion shows go to Galeries Lafayette, 40, Bvd Haussman (Chaussée d'Antin metro), while if you need a break from shopping, there is a fantastic view from the rooftop café at the art nouveau department store, La Samaritaine, 19, Rue de la Monnaie (Pont-Neuf metro). Perfume lovers will be in heaven in the huge perfume department at Printemps, 64, Boulevard Haussmann (Havre-Caumartin metro) which also boasts a wide selection of top designer fashion.

Forum des Halles, Rue Rambuteau (Les Halles metro). This is the Parisian equivalent of Covent Garden, a four-storey glass, modern shopping centre, built on the old site of a wholesale fruit and vegetable market. Inside this subterranean shopping centre, you will find over 180 boutiques, mainly selling clothes. There is also a cinema, a swimming pool and a museum.

Markets: You could spend a very enjoyable day indeed just wandering the Parisian markets. My personal favourite is the giant fleamarket, Marché aux Puces St Ouen (Porte de Clignancourt metro) which has over 3,000 stalls, divided between five separate markets on adjoining streets.

The Latin Quarter: This is a popular area for students and young Parisians. In Boulevard St-Michel (St-Michel metro) you will find arty clothing, bookshops and record stores. Also in this area is the picturesque open air market La Mouffe (Monge metro) located in the bottom half of the medieval street, Rue Mouffetard.

St-Germain-des-Près (St-Germain metro): This small, lively area on the Left Bank, near the Latin Quarter, is a fashionable place to shop. Here you will find smart little art galleries, antique shops, bookshops and trendy clothes boutiques. It is a wonderful area just to stroll around window shopping or to sit in the street cafés (*see pages 241–2*).

Four famous landmarks

The Eiffel Tower, Quai Branley (Trocadero metro): Built in 1889 for the World Fair, on the centenary of the Revolution, this 300-metre iron structure has become one of the main symbols of Paris. From the top, the views are spectacular, covering over 40 miles on a good day. As this is one of the most popular tourist attractions in Paris (four million visitors go up to the top each year), be prepared to queue.

Arc de Triomphe, Place Charles de Gaulle (Etoile metro): Another Parisian symbol that we all know so well. It was commissioned in 1806 by Napoleon I in honour of the Grand Army, although he never actually saw it completed. Underneath the monument is the Tomb of the Unknown Soldier in commemoration of all those who died in the First World War. You can pay to go up to the platform at the top which gives a brilliant view of the 12 avenues spanning out around it.

Notre-Dame, Place du Parvis (Cité metro): This stunningly beautiful gothic cathedral has been rebuilt several times since its foundations were laid in 1163 by Pope Alexander III. It suffered greatly in the Revolution, when it was used as a wine store, but survived the Nazi occupation by having all its beautiful stained-glass windows carefully removed for safekeeping. The original rose windows are absolutely spectacular.

Sacré-Coeur, 35, Rue Chevalie de la Barre (Abbesses metro): The foundations of this famous white-domed church were laid in 1870. You can either take the funicular railway or walk to the top for another breathtaking view of the city.

Culture vultures

The selection and quality of museums in Paris is outstanding. State-owned museums such as The Louvre are closed on either Mondays or Tuesdays and offer free admission on Wednesdays or Sundays. The best time to tour the museums is at weekday lunchtimes (apart from Wednesday if there is free admission) as they are usually less crowded then. You can check opening hours of museums in *Pariscope*, a weekly listings magazine.

Below is a selection of some of the most interesting museums in Paris. If you plan to spend the whole day touring museums you can buy a Museums and Monuments card for 55F which gives you entry to 63 museums and monuments in Paris and enables you to jump the queues. Cards are available from Association Inter-Musées, 25, Rue du Renard 75004 Paris (Tel: 42 77 12 33).

Georges Pompidou National Art and Culture Centre, Rue Rambuteau and Rue St-Merri (Rambuteau or Hôtel-de-Ville metros). Closed on Tuesdays.

Also known as the Beaubourg, the Pompidou Centre is the sort of place you instantly either love or hate. Its famous inside-out architecture features a futuristic escalator (expect to queue) up the outside of the building. From the cafeteria at the top, there is a superb view of the city, while on the fourth floor, you will find the National Museum of Modern Art which exhibits art from 1905 to 1965, including works by Picasso, Henri Rousseau, Dali, Matisse, Mondrian, Kandinsky and Magritte. On the third floor, you will find contemporary paintings (1965 onwards) – these are varied two or three times a year to give younger artists a chance of becoming better known.

This lively art centre also houses a cinema, an industrial design area and a photographic gallery. Outside on the cobbled terrace, there is always a colourful selection of jugglers, fire-eaters, acrobats and street performers, as well as a children's workshop (*see page 244*).

Science Museum (La Cité des Sciences et de l'Industrie), Parc de la Villette, 30, Ave Corentin-Cariou (Porte de la Villette metro). Closed on Mondays.
Located in this 55-hectare park, the Science Museum is a fascinating place for both adults and children. Built in 1986, the futuristic interior of the museum is quite spectacular and is designed like a scientific playground in which you explore and participate rather than just view exhibits.

Experience weightlessness on a trip into space, watch a film inside a hemispherical cinema housed in the spectacular space-age "Geode" theatre, or play with some of the many video games and gadgets. There is so much to experience in this museum that you could easily spend at least half a day there.

English brochures and cassettes are available. There is also an Inventorium which runs "discovery" sessions for children (*see CHILD'S PLAY, page 243*).

Musée du Louvre, Rue de Rivoli (Palais Royal or Louvre metro). Closed on Tuesdays.

The foundations of this building were laid by Philip Augustus and the palace was first opened to the public in 1793, four years after the Revolution. It now houses hundreds of thousands of works of art including such world-famous masterpieces as the Mona Lisa and Venus de Milo. Due to the size of the museum, you could easily spend several days here. If you only have a few hours, it is best to buy an English guidebook so that you can decide which sections are of most interest to you. The collections include Egyptian Antiquities, Oriental Antiquities, Greek and Roman Antiquities, Objets d'Art and an enormous collection of paintings from all the European schools (English, Italian, French, Flemish, Dutch, German and Spanish) but predominantly French.

The main entrance to the museum is in the controversial glass pyramid, designed by Pei and erected in the centre of the Cour Napoleon in 1988.

Musée d'Orsay, 1, Rue de Bellechasse (Solferino metro). Closed on Mondays.

This relatively new museum opened in 1986, converted out of a disused railway station which was originally designed by Laloux in 1900. The collections here span from the late 1840s to 1914 and aim to cover the gap between what you will find at the Louvre and at the Pompidou Centre. Here you will find the main collection of Impressionist art in Paris as well as a superb display of art nouveau.

Musée Picasso, Hôtel Sale, 5, Rue de Thorigny (St Paul metro). Closed on Tuesdays.

This museum is housed in one of the finest former private residences of the "Marais" district and comprises the largest single collection of Picasso's paintings, sculptures and personal memorabilia.

Musée de l'Orangerie, Place de la Concorde (Concorde metro). Closed on Tuesdays. The *Water-Lilies* galleries are sometimes closed in the lunch hour.

Claude Monet enthusiasts will love this small airy museum which exhibits Monet's *Water-Lilies*, eight huge compositions painted at Giverny between 1915 and the artist's death. Upstairs the Jean Walker and Paul Guillaume collection includes work by Sisley, Cezanne, Renoir, Picasso, Matisse, Rousseau and Modigliani.

Coach Tours

If you are unlucky enough to choose a rainy day in Paris, one of the best ways to sightsee and stay dry is to go on an organised coach tour. This is also a good way to get a feel for how the city is laid out as most tours last about two hours and cover all the major sites. English commentaries (usually prerecorded) are available.

Try Paris Vision, offering tours of Paris, as well as excursions to places reviewed in this chapter such as "Fontainebleau and Barbizon", "Chantilly" and "Vaux-le-Vicomte and Fontainebleau" (coaches depart from 214, Rue de Rivoli Tel: 42 60 30 01) or Cityrama, departing from the Cityrama bus stop, 4, Place des Pyramides (Tel: 42 60 30 14).

River rats

One of the most romantic and rewarding ways to see Paris is by boat. This is a good way to get your bearings and discover where the famous landmarks are. It is also fun for children. English-speaking commentaries are available.

Les Vedettes du Pont Neuf (Tel: 46 33 98 38), Pont Neuf metro. A one-hour boat trip from Nôtre Dame to the Eiffel Tower and back. An English-speaking commentary is available and boats leave from behind the equestrian statue in the middle of the Pont Neuf bridge. Children can go on this trip unaccompanied at parents' discretion.

Bâteaux-Mouches, Pont de l'Alma (Tel: 42 25 96 10). Alma-Marceau metro. Lunch, tea and candle-lit dinner cruises are available.

Strollers and café lizards

One of the best ways to get the real flavour of Paris is to spend a couple of hours just strolling around the streets. Below are some of the most interesting areas for exploring on foot.

The most pleasant way to rest your feet afterwards is to sit and relax in a café, a perfect place for watching people. Be warned, however, about the Parisian scale of charges. Drinks are often priced according to where you consume them; the cheapest is at the counter, the most expensive is sitting on the terrace (prime spot for people-watching). Nearly all Parisian cafés serve coffee, alcohol, sandwiches and snacks, so once you have a table you can happily sit there for an hour or two and just watch the Parisian world walk by.

Montmartre (Anvers metro): Montmartre automatically conjures up images of dance shows and the can-can captured on canvas by Toulouse-Lautrec, and it is still a very popular place with painters, poets, writers, musicians and actors. Today the main tourist attraction at Montmartre is the Sacré-Coeur (*see page 236*) although it is worth visiting this hilly village just to wander around the picturesque streets and soak in the bohemian atmosphere.

Don't linger too long at the over-commercialised Place du Tertre where dozens of artists clamour to paint your portrait and overpriced restaurants cash in on the popularity of the square. It is much more interesting to explore the quieter backstreets where you will find peaceful little squares, cobbled alleyways and village houses which actually have front gardens (very unusual for Paris!). Place Émile-Goudeau has always been a favourite spot with artists, including Picasso and Matisse, and this is a good place to sit in a café and watch the arty world go by.

Not far from Montmartre, at the bottom of the hill, you will find Pigalle (Pigalle metro), the nightlife district of Paris full of neon lights and strip shows. The most famous venue is the Moulin Rouge on the Boulevard de Clichy.

St-Germain-des-Près (St-Germain metro): Located on the Left Bank, this tiny little area is always fashionable and lively both day and night. After strolling around looking at the little galleries and arty shops (see above), take a seat on the terrace at Les Deux Magots, 6, Place Saint-Germain-dès-Pres or Café Flore, 172, Boulevard

Saint-Germain. Just around the corner from each other, both of these are famous literary cafés which writers such as Gide, Sartre and Hemingway used to frequent.

Montparnasse (Vavin metro): This is still the heart of Parisian café society with famous places such as La Coupole, 102 Boulevard Montparnasse, a stylish art deco restaurant which still holds tea dances, the traditional Le Select, 99 Boulevard Montparnasse, and La Rotonde, 105 Boulevard Montparnasse where the names of famous people who used to go there including Lenin and Trotsky are immortally inscribed on the menu.

The Champs-Elysées (Charles de Gaulle Etoile metro for the Arc de Triomphe end): A stroll along the Champs Elysées is almost a must on a first-time visit to Paris. This wide avenue has sadly lost its former grandeur and is now packed with fast food restaurants and neon signs. There is, however, so much history attached to the Champs-Elysées that it will always be a great landmark of the city. Marie-Antoinette and Louis XVI were just a couple of the people executed here in the Revolution, while Hitler marched his army down this long avenue in 1940, only for the French to celebrate victory there a few years later.

A walk down the Champs-Elysées will enable you to see many major sights including the Arc de Triomphe, the Eiffel Tower and the Place de la Concorde. You can then continue through the Jardin des Tuileries where you will find the Orangerie Museum, and then the Louvre.

Child's play

Paris is is not usually associated with being a place for children, but there is actually plenty for them to do and see. Below are some suggestions.

The Parisian Circus (Cirque de Paris), Avenue de la Commune-de-Paris, Nanterre (RER Nanterre Ville): Located on the outskirts west of Paris, what makes this circus particularly unusual and appealing to children is that they can spend a day there actually participating in learning the skills of the circus. They can be made up like a clown, learn how to juggle or walk a tightrope. A day's ticket includes participation workshops, lunch with the circus artists and a show in the afternoon. Adults are also welcome.

Children's Playground (Jardin des Enfants), 105 Rue Rambuteau (Les Halles metro): If your children are nagging you because they are bored of the Pompidou Centre or shopping at Les Halles, pacify them by taking them to this supervised open-air adventure playground for 7–11 year olds. Group activities are organised or children can play on their own. Parents are only allowed in on Saturdays when they can bring younger children.

Jardin d'Acclimatation, Bois de Boulogne (Porte Maillot metro): If you feel like spending an afternoon relaxing in the fresh air, the Bois de Boulogne is the prefect spot for families. There are all sorts of sports facilities in the park including a free roller-skating rink, a jogging track and bicycles for hire. The Jardin d'Acclimatation is a special pleasure park for children. The most enjoyable way to get there is chugging through the woods aboard the "pleasure train" which departs from near the Porte Maillot metro entrance. Inside the turnstiles, you will find a zoo, a puppet theatre, a playground for the under–12s, a hall of mirrors, dodgem cars, a mini-motorcycle course, donkey rides and boat trips down the "enchanted river".

Science & Technology Museum (Cité des Sciences et de l'Industrie), Parc de la Villette, 30, Ave Corentin-Cariou (Porte de la Villette metro): This museum is lots of fun for all the family (*see CULTURE VULTURES above*). The Inventorium (L'Inventorium) is a special section for children which runs 90-minute discovery sessions. Here children can learn about science through play. Adults are only allowed in when accompanied by children!

The Waxworks (Musée Grevin), 10, Boulevard Montmartre (Rue Montmartre metro): Learn some of the grim details of the French Revolution and see lifelike models of pop stars, film stars and politicians.

Children's Workshop (Atelier des Enfants), Centre Georges Pompidou (Châtelet or Les Halles metro): If you want to tour the Pompidou Centre you can leave children over five on a Wednesday or Saturday to participate in supervised activities, games, painting and sculpture. Children who do not speak French may feel a little lost here, though.

The Cousteau Oceanic Park (Parc Océanique Cousteau), Forum des Halles. (Châtelet or Les Halles metro): Explore the depths of the ocean through audio-visual experience.

Zoo de Vincennes, 53, Avenue de Saint Maurice (Porte Dorée metro): Instead of being in cages, most of the animals here are separated from the public by high walls and moats. There is also a miniature train that tours around the zoo and park. Afterwards you can go for a boat trip on the lake.

The Sewers of Paris (Les Egouts de Paris), Place de la Résistance (Alma Marceau metro): If your children are into bad smells and squalor, they may find an organised tour of the Parisian sewers fascinating!

Further information:
Central Tourist Information Office, 127, Avenue des Champs-Elysées (Tel: 47 23 61 72). Etoile or George V metro. The place to pick up brochures, maps and tourist information about Paris.

EXCURSION SEVEN: VAUX-LE-VICOMTE

Distance from Euro Disney:
44 km.

Directions from Euro Disney:
Drive west A4 towards Paris, exit Emerainville/Melun (N104) and drive to Melun, then take N36 and follow signs to Vaux-Le-Vicomte.

Why go to Vaux-le-Vicomte?
- To see the inspiration behind Versailles.
- A less touristy alternative to Versailles.
- As a combined excursion with Fontainebleau (*see page 219*).
- To tour the beautiful gardens.

Description
This fairytale château dates back to the 17th century when it was built for Nicolas Fouquet, Superintendent of the Treasury and one of the wealthiest men in France. He used three of France's most talented men to build Vaux-le-Vicomte, the architect Louis Le Vau, the painter Charles Le Brun and the landscape gardener André Le Nôtre.

In 1661, Fouquet hosted the most lavish party ever given at the château and invited the young king of the time, Louis XIV. Unfortunately, the splendour of the occasion evoked the King's jealousy and a few weeks later he had Fouquet arrested and charged with swindling the treasury funds.

With Fouquet behind bars, Louis XIV now set about building an even grander château and commissioned Le Vau, Le Brun and Le Nôtre to set to work on Versailles.

Vaux-le-Vicomte was sold by Fouquet's widow before it was finished. Today you can see the unfinished work of Le Brun in the Grand Salon. The estate was bought in 1875 by the Sommier family who saved and restored this magnificent château and gardens.

A tour around the interior of the château is fascinating and the grounds, with their sculpted hedges, pools and fountains, are truly stunning. There are also fountain displays on the second and last Saturday afternoons of every month.

Further information:
Vaux-le-Vicomte 77950 Maincy (Tel: 60 66 97 09).
Closed during December and January.

CHAPTER TWELVE

THE UNOFFICIAL DISNEY QUIZ

Below are questions to test you and your family's knowledge of the wonderful world of Disney.

1. Which was the first Walt Disney sound cartoon?
2. What is the man-cub called in *The Jungle Book*?
3. Where and when did Disneyland open?
4. Which was the first full-length animated feature film?
5. What was the original name intended for the famous Disney mouse?
6. Who taught Dumbo to fly?
7. What is the name of Mickey's girlfriend?
8. What are the names of Donald Duck's nephews?
9. What character starred as the Sorcerer's Apprentice in *Fantasia*?
10. What sort of animal is Uncle Scrooge?
11. What colour of nose does Chip have?

12. What colour of nose does Dale have?
13. What is Walt Disney's middle name?
14. When was Walt Disney born?
15. What did Disney win his first Academy Award for?
16. In what year did Walt Disney die?
17. When did the EPCOT centre open at Walt Disney World Resort?
18. When did Tokyo Disneyland open?
19. When did Disney-MGM Studios open at Walt Disney World Resort?
20. Who is Ariel's crabby friend?
21. In which cartoon do Figaro and Cleo feature?
22. Who is in charge of the *Nautilus*?
23. Who was born on 18 November 1928?
24. In which film did the calypso song *Under the Sea* feature?
25. Complete the wicked queen's question of her mirror "Magic mirror on the wall . . ."
26. From the basement of which New York landmark did the International Rescue Aids Society in *The Rescuers* operate?
27. In which year was *Bedknobs and Broomsticks* released?
28. Who gets wet in an *April Shower*?
29. Mickey Mouse co-starred with which Disney favourite in no less than 26 cartoons between 1935 and 1932?
30. What type of accent does Disney's Scrooge have?
31. What do the Dwarfs sing on their way home from work?
32. Who played the part of Pinocchio's conscience?
33. Which actor and actress bobbed along at the bottom of the beautiful briny sea?

THE UNOFFICIAL DISNEY QUIZ

34. Which classical composition inspired the vision of Mount Olympus in *Fantasia*?
35. Can you name all Seven Dwarfs?
36. Who plays Cratchit in Mickey's *Christmas Carol*?
37. Who gave Hitler the Bronx cheer in Disney's wartime propaganda feature *Der Fuehrer Face*?
38. Which song and which film are the following lyrics from: "I've seen a peanut stand, I've seen a rubber band..."
39. Which film was based on the Joel Chandler Harris *Uncle Remus* stories, starring Br'er Fox?
40. What did the queen order the huntsman to do to Snow White?
41. Who was the leader of the pack of wolves in *The Jungle Book*?
42. In which film did the fierce cat Lucifer terrify the white mice?
43. What does the queen poison Snow White with?
44. Whose play provided the inspiration for the 1951 Disney movie *Peter Pan*?
45. Which animated feature used CinemaScope (using a wider than usual screen) for the first time?
46. How do Perdita and Pongo broadcast their news in *101 Dalmatians*?
47. Which Disney feature had a titanic dragon fight for a climax?
48. What was the name of the brother of albatross Orville, who appeared in the movie *The Rescuers Down Under*?
49. Who tells the dwarfs that Snow White has been poisoned?

50. Which band leader-singer was cast as the bear Baloo in *The Jungle Book*?
51. Which favourite tale of the French Court in the mid-17th century became a Disney feature in the 1990s?
52. What was the last animated feature in which Walt Disney took part?
53. How many Oscars has Walt Disney won?
54. From which feature film is this line taken: "Whoso pulleth out this sword . . . is rightwise King of England"?
55. How did the Prince awaken Snow White?
56. What was the name of the shy janitor who helped Bianca in *The Rescuers*?
57. Which hero of classic English folklore portrayed in a classic Disney feature has also been played by Errol Flynn and Kevin Costner?
58. Who started his career with Disney before leaving to become director of *Beetlejuice, Batman* and *Edward Scissorhands*?
59. On which fictional English character was the hero of the *The Great Mouse Detective* based?
60. What did Snow White find upstairs in the dwarfs' cottage?
61. Pop stars Bette Midler, Billy Joel and Cheech Marin supplied the voices for which Disney feature based on a Charles Dickens novel?
62. How do the Dalmatian puppies disguise themselves in order to escape?
63. In which country was the sequel to *The Rescuers* based?
64. Where in Euro Disney will you find 999 grisly ghouls?
65. How does the queen disguise herself when she comes to poison Snow White?

66. Who was the purringly evil tiger in *The Jungle Book*?
67. In which Disney film was the Busby Berkeley production number *Be Our Guest* featured?
68. According to Charles Perrault's 17th-century tale, what is the name of the Sleeping Beauty?
69. How many puppies do Perdita and Pongo have?
70. Who made his debut in the 1934 Silly Symphony, *The Wise Little Hen*?
71. Which cartoon features *When You Wish Upon A Star*?
72. What is the name of Baloo's sure-fire musical hit in *The Jungle Book*?
73. Which of Mickey's bashful pals is often heard to exclaim "Gawrsh!"?
74. The eerie Skull Rock overshadows which famous Euro Disney attraction?
75. Fifi the Peke and Dinah the Daschund were wooed by which of Mickey's pals?
76. Who had a sister named Dumbella?
77. Who were the two pesky chipmunks who plagued Donald Duck and later starred in their own series?
78. Who is Anita's horrible friend in *101 Dalmatians*?
79. What is the name of the main thoroughfare through Euro Disney?
80. How many steam trains leave Main Street Station in Euro Disney for a grand tour?
81. Veteran American comedian Bob Newhart supplied the lead voices for the same character in which two Disney features?
82. Where in Euro Disney can you be entertained by can-can dancers?

83. Which Euro Disney hotel boasts an ice-rink in winter?
84. Who lived with Roger Radcliff before he got married?
85. The "How To..." series of cartoon shorts which ran until the mid–1950s were the star vehicle for whom?
86. Who wrote the beautiful Sleeping Beauty ballet music which sets the scene inside Euro Disney's Château de la Belle au Bois Dormant?
87. Who was reduced to a mantel clock by the sorceress' spell in *Beauty and the Beast*?
88. What fearsome fire-breathing beast lurks in the dungeon of Sleeping Beauty's Castle?
89. Where can you stay Wild West-style in Euro Disney?
90. What was the name of Anita's Dalmatian?
91. On which day in 1992 did Euro Disney open?
92. What does Cruella De Vil want the Dalmatian puppies for?
93. What does Snow White give each dwarf before they go to work?
94. Who's Afraid of the Big Bad Wolf was the rallying cry of the stars of which 1933 Disney cartoon?
95. How many Dalmatian puppies were stolen?
96. Who wrote the original tale of *The Little Mermaid*?
97. Which animal family originally adopts the man-cub in *The Jungle Book*?
98. What was the name of the bloodhound in the 1930 Mickey Mouse cartoon *The Chain Gang*, who became a Disney regular?
99. Which veteran star of horror films supplied

the voice for the arch-villain Ratigan in *The Great Mouse Detective*?
100. Who taught Mowgli how to survive the jungle?

Answers
1. *Steamboat Willie*.
2. Mowgli.
3. 1955 at Annaheim, California.
4. *Snow White*, released in 1937.
5. Mortimer; Mickey was chosen to please Walt Disney's wife.
6. Timothy the mouse.
7. Minnie.
8. Huey, Louie and Dewey.
9. Mickey Mouse.
10. A duck.
11. Black.
12. Red.
13. Elias.
14. 5 December 1901.
15. *Flowers and Trees*, 1932.
16. 1966.
17. 1982.
18. 1983.
19. 1989.
20. Sebastian.
21. Pinocchio.
22. Captain Nemo.
23. Mickey Mouse.
24. *The Little Mermaid*.
25. "Who's the fairest of them all?"
26. The United Nations Building.
27. 1971.
28. Bambi.

29. Donald Duck.
30. Scottish.
31. "Heigh-ho, heigh-ho, it's home from work we go!"
32. Jiminy Cricket.
33. Angela Lansbury and David Tomlinson (*Bedknobs and Broomsticks*).
34. Beethoven's Sixth Symphony.
35. Doc, Grumpy, Happy, Bashful, Sleepy, Sneezy and Dopey.
36. Mickey Mouse.
37. Donald Duck.
38. *When I see an Elephant Fly*. Dumbo.
39. *Song of the South*.
40. To kill her.
41. Akela.
42. *Cinderella*.
43. A poisoned red apple.
44. James M. Barrie.
45. *Lady and the Tramp*.
46. The twilight bark.
47. *Sleeping Beauty*.
48. Wilbur.
49. The animals.
50. Phil Harris.
51. *Beauty and the Beast*.
52. *The Jungle Book*.
53. 20.
54. *The Sword and the Stone*.
55. With a kiss.
56. Bernard.
57. Robin Hood.
58. Tim Burton.
59. Sherlock Holmes.
60. Seven unmade beds.

61. *Oliver and Co.*
62. They roll in soot so they look like black labradors.
63. Australia.
64. Phantom Manor.
65. As an old woman.
66. Shere Khan.
67. *Beauty and the Beast*.
68. Princess Aurora.
69. Fifteen.
70. Donald Duck.
71. Pinocchio.
72. *The Bare Necessities*.
73. Goofy.
74. Pirates of the Caribbean.
75. Pluto.
76. Donald Duck.
77. Chip an' Dale.
78. Cruella De Vil.
79. Main Street USA.
80. Three.
81. *The Rescuers* and *The Rescuers Down Under*.
82. The Lucky Nugget Saloon in Frontierland.
83. Hotel New York.
84. Pongo.
85. Goofy.
86. Tchaikovsky.
87. Cogsworth.
88. A dragon.
89. Hotel Cheyenne.
90. Perdita.
91. 12 April.
92. To make fur coats out of their beautiful skins.
93. A kiss.
94. *The Three Little Pigs*.

95. 99.
96. Hans Christian Andersen.
97. The wolves.
98. Pluto.
99. Vincent Price.
100. Baloo.

CHAPTER THIRTEEN

WHERE TO FIND YOUR FAVOURITE DISNEY CHARACTERS

From the moment you walk through the gates, you will have plenty of opportunities to meet your favourite Disney characters. They will happily shake your hand and pose for photos with you and your children.

Young children will particularly enjoy the Disney Parade and the Main Street Electrical Parade where they can see so many of their favourite characters such as Mickey Mouse, Baloo, Cinderella, Goofy (Dingo, in French), Donald Duck, Pluto, Roger Rabbit and Chip and Dale (Tic et Tac, in French). Other good places to meet the Disney characters include at the special character breakfasts in the top hotels, and at the C'est Magique show on Fantasy Festival Stage.

In this chapter, we will tell you which rides and attractions feature certain characters.

We have included their "date of birth" which refers to when the Disney characters originated. Many of them are actually a lot "older" as they are derived from classic stories and plays.

Name: **ALICE**
In French: Alice
Date of birth: 1951 in the Disney cartoon, *Alice in Wonderland*, based on Lewis Carroll's story.
Where to find Alice in Euro Disney: Alice's Curious Labyrinth (Fantasyland)
Characteristics: Pretty little blonde girl, famous for her Alice band.

Name: **BASHFUL**
In French: Timide
Date of birth: Christmas 1937 in the film *Snow White and the Seven Dwarfs*.
Where to find Bashful in Euro Disney: Snow White and the Seven Dwarfs (Fantasyland)
Characteristics: Bashful expression, bulbous nose, broad cheeks and white beard. Wears a long cap.

Name: **CAPTAIN HOOK**
In French: Capitaine Crochet
Date of birth: 1953 in the film *Peter Pan*, based on J. M. Barrie's play.
Where to find Captain Hook in Euro Disney: Peter Pan's Flight (Fantasyland).
Characteristics: A metal hook for his left hand which was eaten by a crocodile.

Name: **CHESHIRE CAT**
In French: Chester
Date of birth: 1951 in the film *Alice in Wonderland*
Where to find the Cheshire Cat in Euro Disney: Alice's Curious Labyrinth.
Characteristics: Huge beaming smile.

WHERE TO FIND YOUR FAVOURITE CHARACTERS

Name: **CLEO**
In French: Cleo
Date of birth: 1940 in the film *Pinocchio*, based on the tale by Carlo Collodi
Where to find Cleo in Euro Disney: Pinocchio's Adventures (Fantasyland)
Characteristics: A goldfish.

Name: **DOC**
In French: Prof
Date of birth: Christmas 1937 in the film *Snow White and the Seven Dwarfs*.
Where to find Doc in Euro Disney: Snow White and the Seven Dwarfs (Fantasyland).
Characteristics: Pompous, self-appointed leader of the Seven Dwarfs. Broad cheeks, bulbous nose, white beard and wears a long cap.

Name: **DOPEY**
In French: Simplet
Date of birth: Christmas 1937 in the film *Snow White and the Seven Dwarfs*.
Where to find Dopey in Euro Disney: Snow White and the Seven Dwarfs (Fantasyland).
Characteristics: Human with the mannerisms and intellect of a dog. Shows off with a slaphappy dance. Broad cheeks, bulbous nose and wears a long cap. Doesn't talk.

Name: **DUMBO**
In French: Dumbo
Date of birth: 1941 in the cartoon *Dumbo*.
Where to find Dumbo in Euro Disney: Dumbo the Flying Elephant (Fantasyland)
Characteristics: Baby elephant who learns to fly.

Name: **FIGARO**
In French: Figaro
Date of birth: 1940 in the film *Pinocchio*.
Where to find Figaro in Euro Disney: Pinocchio's Adventures (Fantasyland).
Characteristics: Geppetto's cat.

Name: **GEPPETTO**
In French: Geppetto
Date of birth: 1940 in the film *Pinocchio*.
Where to find Geppetto in Euro Disney: Pinocchio's Adventures (Fantasyland).
Characteristics: Old man, woodcarver and "father" of Pinocchio.

Name: **GRUMPY**
In French: Grincheux
Date of birth: Christmas 1937 in the film *Snow White and the Seven Dwarfs*.
Where to find Grumpy in Euro Disney: Snow White and the Seven Dwarfs (Fantasyland).
Characteristics: Perpetual scowl, broad cheeks, bulbous nose, white beard and long cap.

Name: **HAPPY**
In French: Joyeux
Date of birth: Christmas 1937 in the film *Snow White and the Seven Dwarfs*.
Where to find Happy in Euro Disney: Snow White and the Seven Dwarfs (Fantasyland).
Characteristics: Always smiling. Broad cheeks, bulbous nose, white beard and long cap.

WHERE TO FIND YOUR FAVOURITE CHARACTERS

Name: **JIMINY CRICKET**
In French: Jiminy Criquet
Date of birth: 1940 in the film *Pinocchio*.
Where to find Jiminy Cricket in Euro Disney: Pinocchio's Adventures (Fantasyland).
Characteristics: Little cricket who wears a top hat, white gloves and carries an umbrella. Acts as Pinocchio's conscience.

Name: **MAD HATTER**
In French: Le Chapelier Fou
Date of birth: 1951 in the film *Alice in Wonderland*.
Where to find the Mad Hatter in Euro Disney: Mad Hatter's Teacups (Fantasyland).
Characteristics: Eccentric character who celebrates "unbirthdays" and loves holding tea parties.

Name: **MONSTRO THE WHALE**
In French: Monstro la Baleine
Date of birth: 1940 in the film *Pinocchio*
Where to find Monstro the Whale in Euro Disney: Pinocchio's Adventures (Fantasyland).
Characteristics: Huge whale which swallows Pinocchio.

Name: **PETER PAN**
In French: Peter Pan
Date of birth: 1953 in the film *Peter Pan*, based on J. M. Barrie's play.
Where to find Peter Pan in Euro Disney: Peter Pan's Flight (Fantasyland).
Characteristics: Little boy in Robin Hood-type costume who can fly and who refuses to grow up.

Name: **PINOCCHIO**
In French: Pinocchio
Date of birth: 1940 in the film *Pinocchio*.
Where to find Pinocchio in Euro Disney: Pinocchio's Adventures (Fantasyland)
Characteristics: Little boy puppet who comes to life and whose nose grows when he tells a fib.

Name: **SLEEPY**
In French: Dormeur
Date of birth: Christmas 1937 in the film *Snow White and the Seven Dwarfs*
Where to find Sleepy in Euro Disney: Snow White and the Seven Dwarfs (Fantasyland)
Characteristics: Droopy-eyed dwarf with broad cheeks, bulbous nose, white beard and long cap.

Name: **SNEEZY**
In French: Atchoum
Date of birth: Christmas 1937 in the film *Snow White and the Seven Dwarfs*.
Where to find Sneezy in Euro Disney: Snow White and the Seven Dwarfs (Fantasyland)
Characteristics: Broad cheeks, bulbous nose that is always twitching, white beard and long cap.

Name: **SNOW WHITE**
In French: Blanche Neige
Date of birth: Christmas 1937 in *Snow White and the Seven Dwarfs*
Where to find Snow White in Euro Disney: Snow White and the Seven Dwarfs (Fantasyland)
Characteristics: Dark hair, fair skin, happy disposition.

WHERE TO FIND YOUR FAVOURITE CHARACTERS

Name: **TINKER BELL**
In French: Clochette
Date of birth: 1953 in the film *Peter Pan*
Where to find Tinker Bell in Euro Disney: Peter Pan's Flight.
Characteristics: Cute little fairy who teaches Peter how to fly.

Name: **WENDY**
In French: Wendy
Date of birth: 1953 in the film *Peter Pan*.
Where to find Wendy in Euro Disney: Peter Pan's Flight (Fantasyland).
Characteristics: Girlfriend of Peter Pan who flies with him to Never-Never-Land.

Name: **WICKED QUEEN**
In French: La Reine
Date of birth: Christmas 1937 in the film *Snow White and the Seven Dwarfs*.
Where to find the Wicked Queen in Euro Disney: Snow White and the Seven Dwarfs (Fantasyland)
Characteristics: Furiously jealous of Snow White's natural good looks. Disguised herself as an old witch and tried to kill Snow White with a poisoned apple.

READERS' RESPONSE

We hope this guide has enabled you to have a thoroughly enjoyable holiday in Euro Disney. If you have any comments about Euro Disney or the content of this book, we would very much like to hear from you. Please send your comments to:

Tania Alexander
c/o Mainstream Publishing
7 Albany Street
Edinburgh EH1 3UG

Index

accommodation 18–19, 35–62
admission charges 33
adults, tours 182–194
Adventure Isle 97–101
Adventureland 70–2; restaurants 139–141; rides and attractions 95–101; shopping 161–2
Alice's Curious Labyrinth 112–4
Annette's Diner 145
Au Châlet de la Marionnette 143
Auberge de Cendrillon 141–2
Auberge du Petit Cheval d'or, Plailly 57
Auberge le Souterrain, Crécy-la-Chapelle 56
auberges 55–8
Autopia (ride) 124–6
Aux Epices Enchantées 140–1

babysitting 76, 178–9
Balladins Hotel, Torcy 52
Base de Plein-Air, Samois-sur-Seine 61
Beaver Creek Tavern 44, 150
Big Thunder Mountain Railroad 83–5
Billy Bob's Bar 148
Billy Bob's Country Western Saloon 178
Blue Lagoon Restaurant 132, 140
Les Bondons, La Ferie-sous-Jouarre 61
booking 27–33
breakfasts 129–130
Buffalo Bill's Wild West Show 178

Cable Car Bake Shop 130, 136
Café de la Brousse 141

267

INDEX

Café des Visionnaires 144
Café Fantasia 39, 149
Café Hyperion 144
California Grill 39, 149
Camp Davy Crockett 48–50, 133, 150
Camp de la Base de Loisirs de Jablines, Jablines 61
camping 48–50, 60–1, 62; restaurants 148–150
Camping d'Île de France, Bois de Boulogne, Paris 62
canoes 88–9
La Cantina 48, 150
Cape Cod 43, 149
Captain Hook's Galley 141
caravan sites 60–1, 62
Carnegie's Deli 132, 145
carts, speciality, for food 130–1
Casey's Corner 131, 136
cash machines 76
cast members 11–12
C'est Magique (show) 175
Champagne region, excursion 215–6

Chantilly, excursion 216–9
character breakfasts 129
characters 260–5
Château de Grande Romaine, Lesigny 59
Château Mortefontaine, Plailly 59–60
châteaux 58–60
Chuck Wagon Café 46, 130, 133, 150
Ciné Magique: Captain EO 120–2
Club Manhattan Restaurant 41, 132, 149
The Coffee Grinder 136
Cookie Kitchen 136
costs 17–24, 32–3
Cottonwood Creek Ranch 93–4
Cowboy Cookout Barbecue 138
Crockett's Tavern 50, 133, 150

dinner 132–3
disabled facilities 14, 77, 78
Discoveryland 73–4; restaurants 144; rides and attractions 116–126; shopping 163

INDEX

Disney characters 260–5
Disney Parade 174
The Disneyland Hotel 37–9
Dumbo the Flying Elephant (ride) 109–110

English language 12
entertainments 174–180
entry charges 32–3
Euro Disneyland Railroad 80–2
excursions 215–247
Explorer's Club 132, 139–140

family tours 194–205
Fantasia Gelati 143
Fantasia in the Sky (fireworks display) 175
Fantasyland 72–3; restaurants 141–4; rides and attractions 101–116; shopping 162–3
Festival Disney 74–5; bars 148; night entertainment 177–8; restaurants 145–150; shopping 163–5

fireworks display 175
first aid 77
Fontainebleau, excursion 219–222
Frontierland 69–70; restaurants 137–9; rides and attractions 83–94; shopping 160
Fuente del Oro 138

Inventions 39, 149
It's A Small World! (boat ride) 114–6

keel boats 87–8
Key West 132
Key West Seafood 146

Lancelot's Carousel 108–9
Last Chance Café 138–9
layout 65–78
Los Angeles Bar and Grill 147
lost children 77
Lucky Nugget Saloon 132, 137
Lucky Nugget Show 176–7
lunches 130–2

Mad Hatter's Teacups 111–2

INDEX

Main Street Electrical Parade 175

Main Street USA 66–9; restaurants 133; rides 80–3; vehicles 82–3

March Hare Refreshments 143

Mark Twain and Molly Brown Steamboats 85–6

Market House Deli 135

money, currency exchange 67, 76

motels 51–4

Newport Bay Club 41–3, 127, 147

The Old Mill 144

opening times 33

Orbitron 123–4

package tours 19, 31–2

Parc Asterix (theme park), excursion 222–31

Parc de la Colline, Torcy 60

Parc de Loisirs de Torcy (theme park), excursion 231–2

Parc Pré Saint Jean, Crécy-la-Chapelle 60–1

Paris: accommodation 61–2; for children 243–5; excursions 232–245; places to visit 233–245; shopping 233–5

parking 27–8

Parkside Diner 41, 130, 149

Peter Pan's Flight 106–7

pets 77

Phantom Manor (ride) 90–2

photographers, tours 207–210

Pinocchio's Adventures (ride) 104–6

Pirates of the Caribbean (ride) 95–7

Pizzeria Bella Notte 131, 142

Le Plat d'Etain, Jouarre 55

Plaza Gardens 130, 131, 134–5

queues 14

quiz 249–258

rain, tours 210–2

Les Relais Bleus, St

Thibault-des-Vignes 51–2
restaurants 128–150
Resthotel Primevère, Meaux Beauval 52
rides 80–126
River Rogue Keel Boats 87–8
Rock Shock (revue) 176
Rustler Roundup Shootin' Gallery 92–3

Self-Catering Rothray, Paris 62
Sequoia Lodge 43–5, 150
shooting gallery 92–3
shopping 152–171; best buys 166–171; best shops 153–5; in Paris 233–5; prices 152
Silver Spur Steakhouse 137–8
Sleeping Beauty (entertainment) 176
Sleeping Beauty's Castle 101–2
snacks 21–4, 136–7
Snow White and the Seven Dwarfs (ride) 103–4
souvenirs 152–171
Sports Bar 148
Star Tours (ride) 116–8

The Steakhouse 147
steamboats 85–6
street performers 177
Swiss Family Robinson Treehouse 99–101

teenagers, best attractions 205–6
tickets 32–3, 65
Toad Hall Restaurant 143
toddlers, best attractions 206
tours: adults 182–194; families 194–205; photographers 207–210; unofficial guide 182–212; when raining 210–2
travel 27–33
Treasure Island 97–9

Vaux-Le-Vicomte, excursion 245–7
Victoria's Homestyle Cooking 131, 135
Le Visionarium 118–120

Walt's 132, 133–4
Walt's Terrace 131
weather 12–13

The Yacht Club 43, 149